The Abuse of Older People
A Training Manual for Detection and Prevention

of related interest

Good Practice in Child Protection
A Manual for Professionals
Edited by Hilary Owen and Jacki Pritchard
ISBN 1 85302 205 5

Good Practice in Supervision
Statutory and Voluntary Organisations
Edited by Jacki Pritchard
ISBN 1 85302 279 9

The Psychology of Ageing
An Introduction 2nd edition
Ian Stuart-Hamilton
ISBN 1 85302 233 0

Dementia
New Skills for Social Workers
Edited by Alan Chapman and Mary Marshall
ISBN 1 85302 142 3
Case Studies for Practice 5

Ageing, Independence and the Life Course
Edited by Sara Arber and Maria Evandrou
ISBN 1 85302 180 6

The Abuse of Older People

A Training Manual for Detection and Prevention

Second edition

Jacki Pritchard

Jessica Kingsley Publishers
London and Bristol, Pennsylvania

First published as The Abuse of Elderly People: A Manual for Professionals in the United Kingdom in 1992 by
Jessica Kingsley Publishers Ltd
116 Pentonville Road
London N1 9JB, England
and
1900 Frost Road, Suite 101
Bristol, PA 19007, U S A

Second edition 1995

Library of Congress Cataloging in Publication Data
A CIP catalogue record for this book is available
from the Library of Congress

British Library Cataloguing in Publication Data
A CIP catalogue record for this book is available from the British Library

ISBN 1-85302-305-1

Printed and Bound in Great Britain by
Cromwell Press, Melksham, Wiltshire

Contents

Foreword to the first edition 7

Acknowledgements 10

Introduction 11

Part I

1. What is Abuse? 15

2. Recognizing Abuse 28

3. Working with Abuse 49

4. Some Basic Facts 70

5. What it's Like to be Abused 81

Part II. The Exercises

6. What is Abuse?—The Exercises 91

7. Recognizing Abuse—The Exercises 99

8. Working with Abuse—The Exercises 109

9. Professional Dilemmas 117

10. Monday Morning In-tray 122

11. Role Play Exercises 126

12. The Case Conference 136

13. Simulation Exercises 152

14. Scenarios 164

Bibliography   173

Appendix 1. Kent County Council Social
           Services Department
           Practice Guidelines for Dealing with
           Elder Abuse   178

Appendix 2. London Borough of Enfield
           Notes of Guidance (Practice and Procedure)
           Abuse of Vulnerable Adults   184

Appendix 3. A Bodychart   197

Index   199

Foreword to the first edition

One consequence of the present community care policies is greater reliance on the support of families, relatives and neighbours in caring for dependent people in their own homes, who, in earlier times, would have sought, or been referred for, residential care. In respect of frail elderly people, the 'burden' on families and neighbours is increasingly severe, particularly in the context of financial constraints in the public services (home helps, community nurses, social workers, etc), and having regard to the heavy costs of private care.

It is not surprising that, for some carers, the feeling of being overwhelmed by responsibilities leads to loss of patience and even to physical or emotional abuse. In addition, because of their frailty, very old people may become victims of attack for other reasons: their money and possessions may be forcibly taken from them; they may be easy prey to the exercise of co-ercive power of various kinds.

Ensuring appropriate care to elderly people lies within the responsibilities of several agencies and professions, but is the main interest of only a few. The NHS and Community Care Act will give weight to the co-ordinating role of care managers in the pursuit of good services; but many professionals undertaking this role would readily acknowledge their lack of expertise in situations of elderly abuse. Certainly, one criterion of good service must be the speedy detection of, and protection from, physical and emotional abuse. Better still, good assessment should be able to identify the impending risks.

This handbook is a timely and valuable contribution to the promotion of good service. Its author has a wealth of experience in social work practice; she has developed special interests in the nature, incidence and handling of abusive situations; and her expertise is effectively distilled in the structure and content of this book. It is a unique publication in that, besides identifying the problems and challenges facing domiciliary workers of all kinds, it provides a training package which can realistically be offered within all agencies engaged in this field of work. Following the presentation of each topic, there are exercises and role plays which successfully integrate theory and practice and which can be used in group supervision and in more formally organised training programmes. The book is directly relevant and useful to training courses leading to various professional qualifications, to staff development within agencies, and to post-qualifying studies. It would provide an especially valuable focus for inter-agency and interdisciplinary training. Where group training opportunities are not available, individual readers can gain considerable knowledge and practical expertise by sharing Jacki Pritchard's experiences of how to help and by following the exercises she offers. The case studies and the recorded comments of elderly people themselves are deeply moving and challenging to anyone professing a concern for welfare.

The subject of this handbook is of increasing public importance. Like child abuse at an earlier time, the subject is one which many helpers find incomprehensible and are reluctant to recognise. I warmly recommend this book to all people engaged in the promotion of effective community care.

Eric Sainsbury
The University of Sheffield

This book is dedicated *in memoriam* to C.R. who caused me
to become interested in the abuse of older people

Acknowledgements

This book could never have been written if people had not been willing to share their experiences with me—colleagues, other professionals, victims and abusers.

I would like to thank the Sheffield Family and Community Services Department for allowing me to pursue my interest in abuse of elderly people. Thanks are due in particular to the current Director, Martin Manby, and to the previous Director, Neil Kay. Without their agreement and support I could not have carried out my research study. Special thanks are due to John Pilling who was the person who first gave serious recognition to the problem of abuse and the work I was doing; he showed enthusiasm and encouraged me when obstacles were put in my way.

I would also like to express my gratitude to Professor Eric Sainsbury, whom I have always referred to as 'my sounding board'. Eric has always given me confidence in what I was trying to do. I have greatly valued his help, advice and comments. He has been invaluable in helping me to think things through and in reading the various drafts of written work.

I am indebted to June Leek for typing the manuscript without any complaints in spite of having to decipher illegible handwriting and listen to endless dictaphone tapes.

Finally, thanks to my son, Nathan, for being so patient whilst I have locked myself away in order to produce this book.

Introduction

My interest in abuse of older people developed some years ago while I was working as a generic social worker in a busy area office. I had had several cases where older people were physically abused but it was one specific case that pushed me into wanting to do something about elder abuse. But what? It was at that point that I began to research the subject more closely and systematically. Since then I have continued the research but I have also been teaching various professionals and students in order to raise awareness and to develop good practice.

My aim in writing this book was to produce something practical which could be used by the different professionals who work with older people. In order to raise awareness three questions have to be asked:

What is Abuse?

How Do You Recognise Abuse?

How Do You Work with Abuse?

I certainly do not know all the answers; I am still learning through experience like everyone else. I hope that by raising these three questions in the early chapters and developing the exercises people will be helped to think more about elder abuse and to develop ways of working with abused older people and with the abusers.

Since writing the first edition of this book, I have continued to widen my experience in working with elder abuse through being a manager (who since reorganisation in a local authority social services department has had to manage social workers, home care staff and a residential unit!) and a trainer, but also through acting as a consultant to various local authorities. Consequently, in this second edition I have updated the reader on recent developments in research and practice in working with elder abuse, but I have also added some more exercises and materials which can be used in a variety of settings.

I have given more attention to institutional abuse because I have gained more experience in this area of work, but a supplementary training book for residential staff will become available to use in conjunction with this book. There will also be a supplementary book for home care staff.

The issue of black elders is still not addressed sufficiently, again because of the limited amount of experience. As I have said previously, this is a crucial issue, and one which must be addressed in the future.

Part I

1 What is Abuse?

Definition of abuse:

> 'misuse, perversion; unjust or corrupt practice; reviling; insulting or unkind speech'.

Oxford English Dictionary

Every human being has his or her own set of values and attitudes, which affects his or her behaviour. It is crucial for the professional to be clear in his own mind what abuse means to him. This is particularly important when working with cases of elder abuse. Elder abuse is still very much a taboo subject; professionals and the general public alike either do not believe it exists or refuse to believe that it can exist ('who would want to injure a frail old lady anyway?'). Professionals will come up against much opposition, resistance and criticism when working with elder abuse and it is therefore important that they have previously given thought to what constitutes abuse so that they can argue clearly and succinctly when called upon to do so. Abuse in any sense is a very emotive subject. What may seem abusive to one person may not seem so to another.

Where does the opposition come from?

Elder abuse is an issue which has not been given very much attention in western society and in general people know very little about the subject. It is often easier to believe that something does not exist than to face what may be an extremely shocking truth. Also, there are many obstacles to overcome before this subject will gain its rightful recognition.

Ageism is very much part of our society. Older people are not seen to be important and are certainly not given the same respect as they are in many other cultures. An older person is thought to be of no use once they reach retirement age probably because they are not seen to be producing anything for the society in which they live. They are considered 'to have had their life'—so why should we try to help them? 'Being old' is also a frightening thought to many people and one which they do not want to think about. Consequently, many people choose not to work or mix socially with older people, preferring the company of young children and their families.

Children do have a high profile in our society because 'they are our future' and they tend to be given priority over older people. Social services departments are especially 'guilty' of this because their primary concern is the welfare of the child. Where generic social work practice exists older people are given a low priority and it is only within specialist teams for older people that they are given any recognition or priority. Other agencies can be guilty of the same neglect. At this time of scarce resources and budget constraints it is understandable that some professionals and their agencies will be reluctant to take on another problem which could be like 'opening a can of worms'. However it is an important issue which will have to be addressed in the near future because in this country the population is ageing. The fastest growing sector of the population is the 85+ year-olds and it has been estimated that by the end of the century one third of the population will be aged over 60 years. Both central and local government are going to have to plan for the consequences of this. Older people are likely to be more dependant in their eighties and nineties and will need more resources to help them to achieve a good quality of life.

So what is abuse?

Even researchers who have been working for many years on the subject cannot agree on a straightforward definition. During the past three years I have sat in workshops and conferences where the 'experts' have debated the issue at length and still not produced one definition which satisfies everyone. Unfortunately, I am sure the debates will continue and that it will take many more years, during which there will be both good and bad practice before any meaningful conclusions are reached.

However, it is very important for each individual to be clear what abuse means to him or her. It is not the purpose of this chapter to write a set of definitions or guidelines for the reader's perusal or future use. It is the intention of the author to provoke some initial thinking so that the reader may use the exercises in Chapter 6 to develop his or her own ideas and definitions.

Professionals will come up against opposition in everyday practice. Some people do not believe that older people are abused in the community or institutions; nor do they believe that it is an issue which should be debated. One consultant actually said to me that 'elder abuse does not exist and it is not a problem'. This is extremely difficult to work with and it emphasizes the fact that raising people's awareness is crucial in these situations. Another dimension to the problem is what may present as an abusive situation to one person may not be considered to be abusive to another and this is where professional conflicts arise. On one occasion when I was running a study day, a residential worker in an old people's home disputed every definition of abuse I presented. He said 'everything you've talked about I do to my own parent as well as to the residents where I work. I don't consider myself to be a perpetrator'.

Some behaviour or actions may be perfectly acceptable to one professional but not to another. For example:

- a nurse felt that force feeding was not a form of abuse even if it meant ramming food down the older person's throat. The social worker felt this *was* a form of physical abuse.

- a district nurse believed an old man was being abused by his daughter because he was tied into an armchair all day long and was not allowed to walk with a zimmer frame. The general practitioner said this was acceptable practice because the man wandered about and restricting his movements helped the daughter, who was under stress.

- a social worker did not want to intervene when Mr B continued to physically abuse his wife on a daily basis because 'she's been battered all her life so it doesn't matter'. The home care organizer wanted Mrs B to be offered support and maybe some form of temporary or respite care, as Mrs B could no longer protect herself because she was physically frail and demented.

- a community psychiatric nurse believed she could continue to support an older person in the community but staff at day hospital said the patient needed institutional care.

- a consultant geriatrician supported a niece who wanted her aunt 'put in a home', but the social worker opposed this because the aunt wished to move to sheltered accommodation and be supported by domiciliary services.

- a ward sister wanted to inform the DSS that a long stay patient Miss T was not using all her mobility allowance and therefore 'it should be stopped because she doesn't need it'. The social worker argued that Miss T was entitled to receive this benefit.

Professionals sometimes try to 'explain away' abusive behaviour but the fact still remains that abuse is taking place. We need to ask ourselves whether it is acceptable when:

- a confused older person is drugged to keep them quiet

- a relative takes some of the pension as a reward for all the help he or she gives

- a carer reaches the end of his or her tether and hits the dependent person

- a mentally ill wife starves her husband when she becomes ill

- a son threatens and shouts at his mother because 'it makes her behave herself'

- an older man is locked in a room with only a bed and commode because he is immobile and doubly incontinent

The victim of abuse may be an older person who is considered to be a management problem. Professionals who work in institutions feel that certain practices have to be implemented in order to manage the establishment and safeguard the users of the service, for example, keeping doors locked, waking people up, getting them dressed or putting them to bed at set times of the day, not offering choice of meals or mealtimes, not being able to have personal possessions.

This leads us to the concept of a **professional dilemma.** We all face dilemmas in our lives, but as professionals we also face dilemmas in our working lives. Patricia Riley has defined a professional dilemma as 'a situation in which a person who has specialist knowledge is confronted by choices between equally unacceptable alternatives...dilemmas are about doing and sometimes about not doing' (Riley 1989).

Sometimes life is made a lot easier by choosing to not take any action rather than choosing to get involved, face difficult situations and have to make decisions. Some professionals have admitted to me that they have chosen not to do anything in particular because they have in fact not known what to do. I suspect that this has been particularly true in cases where a professional has suspected that an older person is suffering from some form of abuse. In Chapter 6 I have designed an exercise entitled Professional Dilemmas. The objective of the exercise is to develop an understanding of the concept of a professional dilemma and thereby to improve practice.

When I began my own research into elder abuse I was, in a sense quite naive because I was looking at abuse in a purely physical sense. However, I soon came to realize that this definition was far too narrow; often social workers said such things as 'but he's mentally cruel to her as well' or 'he's neglected emotionally' and such like. It became evident that the older person was suffering from more than one *type* of abuse. Consequently, I adopted Mervyn Eastman's definition of abuse: 'the systematic maltreatment, physical, emotional or financial of an elderly person...this may take the form of physical assault, threatening behaviour, neglect and abandonment or sexual assault', (Eastman 1984 p. 23). Subsequently I have continued to use these three main categories of abuse, i.e. **physical, emotional and financial.**

In recent years, I have been a member of a working party whose brief was to produce guidelines for a local authority Social Services Department and I have acted as consultant to other working parties. This has involved many debates about what constitutes abuse and whether certain types of abuse should be categorized as physical or emotional abuse or both. For example, where does sexual abuse fit in? Should it be a category on its own? Should it come under physical abuse? But there again, it could be considered to be a form of emotional abuse in certain circumstances—such as when a son masturbates in front of his mother.

The same argument applies to neglect. Again neglect could be considered to be physical abuse (for example, a person is not fed properly and as a result suffers from malnutrition and dehydration; someone is not cared for so that they are left smelly and dirty in the same clothes) or emotional abuse (for example, no-one bothers to talk to an older person; a person is told they are 'a nuisance', 'useless', 'mental', 'stupid'). Then there is self neglect. Should this be considered a form of abuse? Medical and nursing staff would probably say that it is, whereas a social worker may argue that if the person is mentally sound it is their own choice to live as they wish.

And the debate goes on. What is very clear, however, is that professionals need some basis from which to start; the implementation of guidelines and procedures can be a useful beginning. When developing guidelines we have to remember that we are dealing with adults, some of whom will be mentally sound and capable of making their own decisions and choices. This is a totally different situation from child abuse, where agencies have statutory obligations to protect children.

Since 1988 more individuals have been undertaking their own research projects regarding elder abuse and gradually it has been recognised that 'neglect' and 'sexual abuse' need to be considered as separate categories of elder abuse. Consequently, it is generally accepted that there are now five main categories of elder abuse:

- physical
- emotional
- financial
- neglect
- sexual.

Recently, the Social Services Inspectorate have put forward a useful definition:

> 'Abuse may be described as physical, sexual, psychological or financial. It may be intentional or unintentional or the result of neglect. It causes harm to the older person, either temporarily or over a period of time.' (Social Services Inspectorate 1993, p.3)

I welcome this definition as it give clear guidance to social services departments, who must take the lead in investigating abuse. Professionals are very well aware that carers in the community do not receive adequate support. But it is also important to recognise that sometimes carers do not receive appropriate advice or education about a particular illness, for example how Alzheimer's Disease can cause a change in personality, or the effects of a stroke. A carer may engage in some activity which s/he thinks is a way of caring for someone, but someone else may think this is a form of abuse.

Case example

Mrs L was obsessional about being tidy. She went to live with her twin sister, Lottie, who had suffered several strokes and was severely demented. Mrs L kept her sister isolated in a small, stark, bedroom, where there was only a hospital bed, commode, and high back chair, which was placed in front of the window. Lottie could only say a few words, so Mrs L did not talk to her. Home care staff came at 8.00 a.m. to wash and dress Lottie, who was then placed in the chair in front of the window until 8.00 p.m. when home care staff came again to put her to bed. When Lottie started going to day centre, she started interacting with users and staff and her speech improved. One day she even got up and walked to the toilet by herself.

This is a classic example of 'unintentional' abuse. Mrs L was caring for her sister in the way she thought was best. No-one had talked to her about the effects of dementia or how her sister's speech could improve if she received attention and stimulation. People like Mrs L need practical help and advice and that is why cases like this must be made a priority within social services departments.

I think the other useful part of the Social Services Inspectorate's definition is its statemeant that abuse may be 'occurring temporarily or over a period of time'. It suggests that even if we think that some incident is 'a one off' we should take it seriously and investigate the situation. This moves us on from Eastman's original conception of 'systematic maltreatment'.

I welcome this guidance as all professionals must take the issue of abuse seriously and confront it head on; *not* sweep it under the carpet. The general public must also be made aware that social workers are not going to be 'heavy handed' in dealing with elder abuse. Because social workers are often seen in a bad light, there is a notion that social workers, when investigating cases of elder abuse, might be taking carers off to the local police station. This is highly unlikely. Social workers must be shown in a positive light, in other words that they are there to understand what is happening and help in some way.

The use of guidelines

Very few agencies have implemented guidelines as policy for working with elder abuse, although in recent years an increasing number of social services departments are giving recognition to the need for procedures, and more working parties have been set up to draw up policies and procedures (see Hildrew 1991).

Many departments, in order to avoid reinventing the wheel, have adopted or adapted the guidelines which were produced by Kent Social Services Department back in 1987. Kent were the pioneers in this field when they produced 'Practice guidelines for dealing with elder abuse', as a result of concern expressed by both fieldwork and residential staff. Once the guidelines were put into use, workers learnt by experience and it was felt that the guidelines needed to be altered and developed further. A second version was produced in July 1989 'to take account of more detailed research and reports improvements in practice systems' (Kent County Council 1989).

The guidelines define abuse as falling within four categories which may be further sub-divided:

1. Physical abuse
    a. medical health maltreatment
    b. bodily impairment
    c. bodily assaults
2. Psychological abuse
    a. humiliation
    b. harassment
3. Sociological abuse
4. Legal abuse
    a. material exploitation
    b. personal exploitation
    c. theft

Kent guidelines are concerned solely with abuse of elderly people. Other authorities, such as the London Borough of Enfield, have produced guidelines which deal more broadly with vulnerable adults (see Appendix 2). One of the aims of the working party set up by the London Borough of Enfield was 'to define abuse of vulnerable adults in its various aspects' (Section 1.3.1). The guidelines explain that:

> the working party examined a number of possible definitions and whether Enfield should have one at all. James Callahan (1986) has argued that any single definition is too restricting and would rule out some important abuse-related facets. Others, however, including the working party, regard this both as evading the issue and causing difficulties in establishing who is excluded/included within any practice guidelines. (Section 2.2).

Subsequently, the following working definition was suggested:

> the physical, emotional or psychological abuse of a vulnerable adult by a formal or informal carer. The abuse is repeated and is the violation by a person/or persons who have power over the life of a dependant. (Section 2.3.1).

This definition is narrow in the sense that it assumes that the carer is the abuser. From my own practical research and experience in Sheffield it seems that older people are not always abused by a carer; abusers may also be someone in the community who is not necessarily a carer or relative but perhaps a neighbour, friend or stranger.

The London Borough of Enfield outlines abuse within the following framework:

1. Physical assault
2. Threats of physical assault/actions
3. Neglect
4. Sexual abuse and interference (threatened or actual)
5. Abandonment to residential care or hospital
6. Exploitation
7. Psychological abuse
8. Denial of basic human rights (Sections 2.6.1 to 2.6.8)

Recently, more local authorities have produced policy or draft guidelines for working with abuse of older people. The turning point seems to have come in 1991. At this time the Association of the Directors of Social Services (ADSS) produced a document 'Adults at Risk' (ADSS 1991) and at the same time the Social Services Inspectorate (SSI) were carrying out research into elder abuse in two London boroughs. Their findings were published in *Confronting Elder Abuse* (SSI 1992), after which three workshops were convened to which all social services departments and health authorities were asked to send a representative to discuss what should be included in national practice guidelines. In 1993 the document *No Longer Afraid: the safeguard of older people in domestic settings* was produced (SSI 1993).

Even now there are considerable variations in the local guidelines which are produced. Some remain simplistic, short and to the point, while others go into great length in the attempt to reach precise definitions. A consensus has not been reached.

Some authorities consider certain forms of abuse to be important enough to be categorized on their own rather than considering them under the general heading of physical abuse (e.g. sexual abuse, neglect, misuse of medication, deprivation of food). Similarly, because emotional abuse is so difficult to define, some authorities categorize forms of this type of abuse under psychological or sociological abuse (e.g. forcible isolation/confinement, humiliation, harassment, bullying, threats, verbal abuse, mental anguish, fear). Financial abuse is also sometimes separated into legal abuse, extortion, material exploitation, personal exploitation, misuse of money/property.

One could spend a great deal of time discussing definitions and it must be noted again that such discussion often generates much heated debate. But it must be emphasized that, for practical purposes, each professional must give thought to the subject and reach their own conclusions and definitions. This was the main objective in designing the exercises outlined in Chapter 6.

Some authorities (such as the London Borough of Enfield) have produced their guidelines in conjunction with other agencies, thereby adopting the multidisciplinary approach. This consensus view is very important because each discipline works in a different way, but again this brings us back to individual attitudes and values. Adopting the multidisciplinary approach often works in theory but in practice it can result in a number of problems.

As professionals we are usually all working towards the same end but we might get there in various different ways. For example, medical and nursing staff have a clinical approach to their work. They are presented with a problem and tackle it in a very practical way. Often the patient is told the opinion of the doctor or nurse. In contrast, social workers are described as being 'wishy washy' because they have a more 'laid-back' approach. They adopt a non-judgmental approach and endeavour to facilitate the client to make his or her own decisions.

Hence, if professional bodies start to produce their own guidelines in isolation, we may never reach any consensus of definition. In 1991 The Royal College of Nursing produced guidelines for its members and its statements define abuse itself rather than listing categories of abuse, which is employing a different methodology:

'...the ongoing inability of an informal carer to respond adequately to meet the needs of a dependent older person. This results in the violation or loss of that person's human rights.'

Abuse is considered to be active or passive:

'Active abuse includes: physical assault, giving inappropriate medication, being verbally or emotionally abusive, sexually abusive, isolating or confining the older person against their will and misusing money or property. Passive abuse includes failure to give prescribed medication or to help in the performance of daily living activities.'

A conclusion is reached in the definition:

'Abuse thus threatens bodily, psychological and social integrity. It may result from a willful desire to cause harm but frequently occurs because the caregiver lacks the necessary strength, will or knowledge to respond to the older person's needs.'

It is extremely important for all professionals to try to develop an understanding of how other professionals work and function in different ways, even when all are trying to achieve the same ends. Exercises in Chapter 6 have been developed to help the reader address these difficulties.

Some basic starting points

Professionals should remember that every older person has rights:

The right to choose

The right to privacy

The right to independence

The right to a decent quality of life

The right to protection and safety

Abuse occurs when a person is deprived of a satisfactory quality of life. But these statements assume that we all have the same standards whereas in fact quality can mean different things to different people. For example, an older woman may be perfectly content living in one room of a house in which she has lived for the past 50 years, even though the walls are damp, the ceiling is crumbling and only one bar of the electric fire is working. What right has anyone to suggest that she should move to a warm, comfortable bed-sit in sheltered accommodation if she does not wish to do so?

Similarly, many older people choose to remain in an abusive situation. What right has any professional to try to remove the person from that situation or even try to persuade them to change their minds? If someone is mentally sound and is capable of making decisions, all a professional can do is to offer support and explain what options are available to that person. However, professional dilemmas arise when somebody is not mentally sound and cannot make rational decisions. Alternatively, an abuser may very well be dementing and may abuse someone they actually care a great deal about. Again, there is a dilemma as to whether professionals should intervene to protect the victim. There are no right or wrong answers. All we can do as professionals is try to do what we think is right and what constitutes good practice. We all make mistakes and we continue to learn by making those mistakes. In working with elder abuse we still have much to think about and learn. Exercises in Chapter 6 look in more detail at the question 'what is abuse?'

2 Recognizing Abuse

In this chapter the reader will not be given magic solutions to the problems of elder abuse. As has already been said, it is a very complex area of work and certainly much abuse remains hidden. It may therefore be very difficult for any professional person to recognize that abuse is taking place. Much more research needs to be undertaken in this area and we still have much to learn. The purpose of this chapter is to raise the reader's consciousness—for example explaining some indications of abuse and situations in which it may occur.

Where does abuse occur?

The first important lesson to be learnt is that elder abuse can happen anywhere; that is to say, there are no social or class barriers. Traditionally, it is thought that it is carers who abuse older people because the stress they are under pushes them to the end of their tethers. It is certainly true that carers do abuse in such circumstances and many examples can be given of such cases.

Case example

Mrs J was 80 years old, suffered from senile dementia and was doubly incontinent. She continually laughed and grunted, which got on her husband's nerves. Mr J was an old man himself, had had cancer removed from his nose and was suffering from secondaries. He lost his temper quickly and used to either shake his wife by the shoulders or elbow her.

However, it is not only carers who do the abusing; in fact, the carer can be the victim rather than the abuser. The carer can be physically abused by the person they are caring for; this is quite a common occurrence when a dependent person has behaviour problems due to dementia.

Case example

Mrs I was the sole carer for her husband, aged 76, who was suffering from dementia. Mr I was physically violent and verbally abusive. He threatened the home helps so they had to go into the house in pairs and they actually saw Mr I hit his wife with a stick.

Carers also experience a great deal of emotional abuse which can take many forms, e.g. verbal insults, threats, humiliation, harassment etc. Carers can experience forms of financial abuse in that many of them are not aware of benefits they are entitled to (e.g. attendance allowance). They do not make a claim and often have to struggle financially.

Physical abuse can occur between married couples. There seems to be two types of marital violence. First, where there has been violence throughout the marriage, this continues in the later years. Some researchers into elder abuse feel these cases should be discounted but I feel that this form of elder abuse needs to be given attention because the victims still need to be given advice and support.

Case example

Mr and Mrs H had been known to their social work assistant for a couple of years. Mr H suffered from dementia, Parkinson's disease and had been physically violent towards his wife throughout their marriage. At first they refused all practical help, e.g. day centre and Mrs H would not talk about the violence she experienced. The situation worsened gradually as diabetic Mrs H was losing her sight and becoming more frail. Mr H was up each night and was becoming more abusive towards Mrs H.

The second type of marital violence in older couples occurs when a role reversal takes place. If a husband who has been violent during the marriage becomes dependent and incapacitated in later years the abused wife can start abusing her husband in order to get her own back.

Case example

For the past five years Mr D had been very frustrated by his illness. He had had a couple of strokes but was mentally alert. He expected his 82-year-old wife, who had arthritis and was very frail, to do everything for him. He had physically abused Mrs D for years but then he pushed her which caused her to break her arm. When she was discharged from hospital she returned home to hit him over the head with her pot.

The concept of 'mutual abuse' is present both in carers' situations and in marital situations. This is where two people involved in a situation abuse each other, perhaps physically, verbally and emotionally. I have chaired a number of case conferences where it has been impossible to ascertain who is the victim and who is the abuser. Often this form of abuse has been going on for many years. Social workers find cases like these very difficult to work with because the people involved are not willing to change and seem in some way to enjoy the relationship they have.

Elder abuse can be linked to a history of child abuse in the family. For instance if the person has been abused physically or sexually as a child by a parent the child may abuse that parent once they are old. Another link is that a person may be abusing both his/her own children at the same time as abusing an older parent.

Case example

Mr A, aged 33, was a very bitter man because his two children were taken into care after he had physically assaulted them and eventually they were placed for adoption. He had been sent to prison and had a history of convictions for grievous bodily harm. When he came out of prison, although he had a flat himself, he went to stay with his 65-year-old mother. Mrs A was an anxious woman who was verging on obesity, which affected her mobility. She used a wheelchair. Mr A had abused his mother physically, verbally and financially.

Because there has been so much emphasis on carers abusing older people it is often difficult for people to think about the fact that elder abuse can be deliberate and pre-meditated for personal gain. I would suggest that this is more common than we think. It is usually linked with the fact that the abuser has some specific problem—personal, psychological, or medical. The most common problems I have come across are alcoholism, gambling and drug abuse.

Case example

Mrs E was 82 years old, deaf and supposed to be senile but the consultant disagreed with this diagnosis. She was abused by her alcoholic daughter who had recently married another alcoholic. The daughter had extravagant tastes in clothes which were bought with Mrs E's money. Mrs E was hit regularly by her daughter and the police became involved when £80 went missing after Mrs E had attended day centre. Mrs E was forced to sleep on the settee whilst her daughter and son-in-law lived with her. When the couple were rehoused they took all the furniture including the fridge and Mrs E was left with only a chair, cooker, pots and pans.

Drug abuse is a growing problem in the United Kingdom, in particular the use of crack, even though this is denied by some agencies. For several years the growing number of young people who have become involved in violence in order to steal money, possessions to finance their 'habit' has been a matter for concern. I have been aware of the problem in my own area where youngsters as young as 13 and 14 are addicted to crack and, as a result of this, crimes against the older people have increased because these youths are abusing their own families, neighbours and strangers. Abuse against older people rarely reaches the national papers but one such case did so recently. A 17-year-old boy:

> '...was found guilty of murdering an 88-year-old woman during a 20-day crime spree against elderly people...Casey attacked, robbed and indecently assaulted at least 20 other pensioners...Police believe the number of his victims could be nearer 60...During his trial Casey claimed he never intended to kill and was desperate for money to buy crack cocaine. Police believe he got away with at least £10,000 during the 20 days.'

> *(The Times, Saturday 17th September 1994)*

A growing concern is the number of older people who are abused by groups of school children or youths in their local community. Older people are vulnerable because they are often living alone and may be handicapped in some way, either mentally or physically.

Case example

Mr P was 63 years old and described as being 'educationally sub-normal'. He was abused physically and financially by four boys aged 11, 12, 14 and 15. A neighbour described the screams heard when the boys used to break into Mr P's house and was convinced that Mr P was being tortured. Urine was thrown over Mr P who suffered severe bruising and cigarette burns. Windows were broken frequently; the housing department put in perspex windows but they were also broken so the house had to be boarded up. Mr P also bricked up the back door himself to try to stop the boys coming in.

Case example

Mr C was mentally handicapped and was unable to speak. He walked about in the local community for a large part of each day and was continually made fun of, shouted at and humiliated by all the local children. They also harassed him when he was in his own house, where he lived alone, by pulling faces at the window.

When I first came across the cases mentioned above, I thought abuse by gangs was something peculiar to the council estate I was working on. However, as my research spread across the city it became very clear to me that this was a problem on many council estates but also in high rise blocks of flats. Once I started talking about my theory of 'gang abuse' at national conferences I learnt that this is a national problem in both rural and urban areas. I believe that gang abuse is another aspect of elder abuse which must be confronted and I have expanded on this theme elsewhere (Pritchard 1993a, 1993b).

This type of abuse is very well organised. The gangs watch the routine of an older person, who is usually housebound. They will sit on a garden wall or a landing for a week and find out exactly what time regular visitors call (e.g. home care staff, district nurse, community psychiatric nurse, relatives) or when the person leaves the home (e.g. to go to day care). They will then break into the house (usually on pension day) and physically and financially abuse the older person.

Sometimes the abuse is organised more subtly, because the young people befriend the older person, who is probably isolated and very lonely. Once they have gained the trust of the older person and can gain entry easily, they will start to steal because they will have found out where the older person keeps his/her money, valuable possessions and so forth.

When I have interviewed the children and youths involved in this type of abuse, they have said they have done for it 'revenge' and 'to get power over an adult', because many of them have been victims of abuse themselves.

So far I have been talking about abuse which happens in the community, but it must not be forgotten that elder abuse can occur in institutions, for example local authority homes, private rest homes, nursing homes, and hospitals. All five categories of abuse can happen in institutions. Very little research has been undertaken on the issue of institutional abuse but it is an issue which will have to be addressed in the future (especially in abuse guidelines!).

Again, people need to have their awareness raised about the different forms of abuse which may exist. Abuse can be happen in all sorts of situations:

- care worker abuses resident
- resident abuses care staff
- resident abuses resident
- visitor abuses resident

People often believe that the 'horror stories do not exist in this day and age', and that television documentaries which do shock people are made for sensationalism. In the work I have undertaken as a consultant and as a trainer in the past two years in different authorities I have seen and heard about many abuse situations, for example:

- residents having communal false teeth
- residents who are doubly incontinent are not dressed from the waist downwards. One care assistant said 'What's the point? We'll only have to keep changing them?'
- a principal followed the practice of sending the wedding rings of residents who were widows to headquarters to be included in their financial assessment, because 'they do not need them anymore'

Bad practices can exist in an institution because of lack of knowledge and training. Staffing issues are crucial here. There are many staff who have been working in the same unit for maybe as long as 20 years and feel that they 'know it all. You can't teach me anything new'. These staff may be very resistant to change and ideas about good practice. This is particularly difficult to address if the head of the unit has also been in the unit for a long time. The head of any unit has a great deal of power and the regime which exists can be difficult to change.

On the other hand, some institutions employ very young staff; this happens particularly in the private sector. People as young as 16 and 17 years of age will go to work for a very low hourly rate of pay, because they cannot claim income support. They are usually willing to work any hours, even night shifts. Through no fault of their own they may have no knowledge of or commitment to working with older people.

It is imperative that *all* staff receive appropriate support and regular training. Staff need to feel valued, but also to feel that they are doing a worthwhile job. This can be very difficult in units where staffing levels are low and staff are only involved in basic care. They often feel frustrated that they cannot do more imaginative work such as formulating detailed care plans, carrying out reminiscence work, spending more time with and talking to residents.

People who work in institutions are 'carers' and may experience the same kinds of stress as carers in the community, in other words having to deal with difficult behaviours and situations. They also experience other stresses in that they may be working long shifts, often in units where there may be high dependency levels (Pritchard 1991).

Causal factors

Usually there is not just one causal factor contributing to elder abuse and so there may be several indicators that abuse is occurring. One indicator or more does not automatically mean that a person is being abused, but it may indicate that that person is at risk.

The following is a list of conditions/factors that may contribute to abuse:

1. Increased dependency—as an older person becomes more dependent, this causes more stress for the people involved in caring for that person.

2. Multiple dependency—in some families a carer is looking after more than one dependent person, for example a mother may have young children herself and also be responsible for caring for a frail parent, or a husband may be caring for his physically handicapped wife plus a dependent mother, or a single parent may have

teenage children a full-time job plus old parents living in the same household.

3. Within the family there has been a history of psychological/psychiatric problems.

4. History of abuse in the family, for example physical or sexual abuse of children or marital violence.

5. History of poor family relationships. Some members of the family find it difficult to communicate either because of events, conflicts or differences which have existed in the past or simply because they do not like each other. If a person finds him or herself having to care for an older relative with whom they have a poor or no real relationship this can cause massive resentment.

6. Environmental problems—a family may be living in very poor or overcrowded housing conditions which causes frustration and tension.

7. Financial problems—the family may be existing on a very low income or state benefits which results in them accruing arrears, debts etc. A dependent older person may add to the financial difficulties (e.g. incontinence causing large expenditure at the local laundrette) if the family are not aware that they are entitled to specific benefits, e.g. attendance allowance (which could be used to purchase an automatic washing machine, tumble dryer, new bedding).

8. The older person may present difficult behaviour or personality problems which increases the stress experienced by the carer(s).

9. The carer may have specific problems, e.g. behavioural, interpersonal, financial.

Stress and carers

I keep referring to the fact that researchers and experts claim that older people can be abused by their carers. This can certainly happen and it is important for professionals to try to understand why and what drives them to the ends of their tethers. Although the carer's actions should not be condoned, it is important to empathize and help the carer to understand what is happening. It is also crucial for the carer to be given the opportunity to express their feelings (e.g. of anger, resentment etc.) and to say that they cannot cope any longer if this is the case.

I have written elsewhere about what some carers said pushed them over the edge (Pritchard 1990b). Five main factors were highlighted:

- Behaviour traits of the older person
- The tasks which had to be performed
- Frustration experienced by the carer
- The carer's sense of isolation
- Lack of services and other support

If carers received more support and resources in the community, the number of older people who may be at risk of being abused would be reduced.

It is also important that professionals are not seen as being 'against' carers. Guidelines can be misinterpreted. One support worker said to me that she believed social workers would misunderstand carers and see them as 'evil people who should be reported to the local police station'. Unfortunately, this view can develop because of the way in which the media report such events as Cleveland, Rochdale, Orkney etc.

The Importance of Social History

In order to recognize abuse it is necessary to make a full assessment of a person's family situation. With the implementation of full needs assessments under the Community Care Act, workers are carrying out more detailed assessments and many workers are finding cases of elder abuse where they did not expect to do so.

A worker should carefully consider the presenting problem(s) but should also look further back, because something which has happened in the past may be the root cause of the current abuse. Therefore, it is very important to construct a social history of both the victim *and* the abuser. We need to know exactly what has happened to both people in the past, so that we can work with them *both* in the future. Elder abuse cases are never simple and straightforward, because often they necessitate the understanding of complex family relationships.

It is often very difficult to get information about what has happened to an abuser in the past. The victim is unlikely to disclose very much unless they have built up a trusting relationship with someone. It is likely to be the home help, district nurse or day centre worker who hears stories about what has happened in the past. These are frequently recounted when engaged in intimate activities such as bathing, or dressing. It is also true to say that disclosures about abuse are given in similar situations.

Reminiscence is an important concept when working with older people and can be a useful way in which a worker can learn a great deal about the type of life a person has experienced and the important events which have occurred during that lifetime. Again, this is crucial in working with both the victim and the abuser.

It is usually very difficult to find out if an older person has been physically or sexually abused as a child as it is not something which is normally talked about with members of the older generations—it is only in recent years that some people feel safe enough to talk about what has happened to them previously. We forget that older people have not been encouraged to vent their feelings and 'you kept things to yourself'. It is just as difficult to find out whether a person is being physically or sexually abused when older because, again, 'such things are not discussed'.

Loyalty also plays a crucial element in working with abuse. Older people are going to be reluctant to disclose about relatives who are abusing them. Many older women also believe they should be 'faithful' in every sense of the word to their husband. This means that many of them will not talk about the violence they have experienced during a long marriage because they would feel disloyal if they were to do so. They feel it is their duty to remain with the husband 'for better for worse'.

There is often too much emphasis on the fact that the victim may have problems; what is ignored is the fact that the abuser may have problems rather than the victim. So what would we like to know about the abuser to form a comprehensive social history?

- basic details/chronological history
- what was s/he like as a child?
- did s/he have development problems?
- how did s/he get on with peer groups?
- what was s/he like in adolescence? (were there particular problems e.g. beginning of offending behaviour?)
- in adulthood has s/he had difficulty in forming relationships?
- are there particular problems now—alcohol abuse, gambling, drug/solvent abuse, mental health problems, financial problems etc?

Abuse can be perpetuated, especially if it is learnt behaviour and thought to be a normal part of everyday life. If a child is brought up in a violent environment s/he is likely to think this is an accepted norm and be violent in adulthood.

So what else should we be looking for?

The most obvious starting point is to look for physical signs of abuse but this is not an easy task. It is often difficult to prove that physical abuse of an older person has taken place, for two reasons. First, the injuries may be hidden and it is not very often that people actually see the body of an older person. Second, an older person can sustain injuries very easily and it is difficult to prove that such injuries have been caused non-accidentally. Third, Table 2.1 shows a list of the sort of injuries which may be sustained as a result of abuse.

Other signs of abuse to watch for concern the person's health and the application of medication. The person may suffer dramatic weight loss or become very frail. This can be due to lack of food and liquid. This form of physical abuse is frequently linked to financial abuse when a person is left without money to purchase the necessities of life.

Table 2.1 Physical Injuries

Injury	Difficulty in ascribing to abuse
Bruises	Usually on parts of the body which are not visible
Fractures	Old bones break very easily
Slap marks	They can vanish quite quickly even before they have been seen by someone else
Kick marks	Frequently on the trunk of the body which is not visible
Black eyes	Can be caused during a fall
Burns	It is easy to claim that cigarette burns have been caused by dropping cigarettes inadvertently
Cuts/lacerations	Can be due to falling

We need to get better at monitoring an older person's health. Cliches are too often used in regard to older people—for example, we accept to readily 'she's frail and elderly'. All professionals must ask more questions. Why is someone losing weight? Is there a medical problem or are they being starved? Is there a problem with the current medication or is it being maladministered?

Case example

Eighty-eight-year-old Mrs H was extremely frail and anaemic. She lived alone but was visited every day by her daughter, of whom she was extremely frightened. Her daughter cashed the pension every week but Mrs H never had any money of her own. There was never any food in the house except a cheese sandwich. The warden challenged the daughter about this and was told 'she gets two cooked meals a week. That's enough'. Mrs H went to luncheon club twice a week.

Physical abuse can take place when a person is given either too much or too little medication. Too much medication may be administered in order to cause drowsiness or prolonged periods of sleep. This is common when an older person has behaviour problems, especially in cases of senile dementia. On the other hand, a crisis may be caused deliberately by withholding medication in order to get the older person out of the home and into hospital.

Historically, neglect was always subsumed under physical abuse, but neglect can also be emotional. A definition of neglect is:

> 'slight, disregard, not paying attention to; leave uncared for; leave undone, be remiss about; omit to do or doing.' (Oxford English Dictionary)

Physical neglect can happen when someone's basic needs are not met, for example: the older person is not washed, dressed; is kept in the same clothes; is dressed inappropriately; is not fed. Emotional neglect involves an older person being ignored or not receiving sufficient attention and stimulation which could help them (e.g. after a stroke when their speech has been affected).

The following may be considered to be indications of neglect:

- Ongoing lack of food or drink
- Smell of urine/faeces
- Older person's mobility is restricted due to lack of aids (e.g. 'can't let her have her own walking frame because she will fall and hurt herself')
- Isolation—the older person is confined to living in a small space (e.g. only allowed in a small bedroom or forced to live in a cupboard with no furniture)
- All social contact is withdrawn.

Case example

Sixty-seven-year-old Mr E who was mentally sound but suffered from Parkinson's disease, was abused physically and emotionally by his wife. His son lived in the same house but had epilepsy and was partially sighted resulting from meningitis. Mr E was left in bed for long periods of time. His bedroom was so cramped there was no space to mobilize properly. He was not fed and his medication was not given at regular intervals or sometimes not at all. He had skin problems due to lack of attention. Mrs E shouted constantly at her husband. She often threatened to kill him and in fact had actually stabbed him seven years before.

Like neglect, sexual abuse was always considered to be a form a physical abuse, but it can also be a form of emotional abuse. Sexual abuse is extremely difficult to detect and can only be proven by a proper medical examination. Few older people are likely to disclose to someone that they are being sexually abused. Again, it is likely to be a home help or district nurse who picks up 'the clues' that sexual abuse is occurring. If a confused older person makes allegations it is unlikely that they will be believed because they are likely to be thought to be 'nutty as a fruit cake'. However, if a person does make a statement about being sexually abused, this should always be investigated in the most sensitive way possible.

Because sexual abuse is such a taboo subject, professionals must be trained to look for indications of sexual abuse such as:

- genital or urinary irritation
- frequent infections (e.g. evidence of vaginal discharge may be found on knickers—home care staff are most likely to pick this up or residential staff when an older person comes in for a temporary/respite stay)
- bleeding (blood can be found on underwear, night clothes—home care and residential staff may play a key role in identifying this)
- bruising on inner thighs
- sexually transmitted diseases
- sudden onset of confusion
- depression
- severe upset or agitation when being bathed/dressed/undressed/medically examined (when the older person has not been like this before)

- conversation regularly becomes of a sexual nature (again this has not happened previously).

It is important for all workers to discuss their suspicions or findings with their line managers. I am aware that many cases have been 'missed' because reports from home care staff have not been followed up. There seems to be a great reluctance to investigate. Many GPs seem to avoid examining older women, for example. Infections are frequently diagnosed (without examination) as being 'thrush' or bleeding is said to be due to 'piles' (again without examination!).

There has been very little research in this country into sexual abuse of older people, but in one study it has been shown that 88 per cent of victims were female, the majority of whom were confused or who had suffered a stroke (Holt 1993).

Cases are found where there has been a history of incest, most commonly between mothers and sons. If the mother becomes confused and does not want sexual relationship anymore, the son may find this hard to understand or will not accept it, so he becomes physically violent and even rapes his mother. The same situation can occur in marriages where one partner (either male or female) does not want a sexual relationship anymore and the other partner refuses to accept this.

We have to remember that it is not just females who are victims of sexual abuse. A problem which I keep coming across is the sexual abuse of isolated gay men. These men are abused by gangs of youths, who 'gang rape' the older man; or by individuals who befriend them. It is very hard to work with these cases as it is sometimes difficult to ascertain whether the gay men are consenting to the sexual activities. Where disclosures have been received, it has been clear that the men have been victims of both sexual and financial abuse.

If there are no physical indications of abuse one should watch for signs of events which happen with regularity:

1. The older person may be constantly requesting help from a person who is considered to be important and has some authority, e.g. requests for the general practitioner to visit when there is no further illness or deterioration in health; frequent phone calls to the social worker, district nurse requesting visits.

2. The carer visits the general practitioner; perhaps with the intention of explaining that s/he is not coping or does not want be the main carer. As most GPs only allocate five or ten minutes for each appointment is a carer really going to open up in that short space of time? This is doubtful and consequently the carer may keep returning to the GP.

3. Visits to the Accident and Emergency department at the local hospital. Closer monitoring needs to take place about how often an older presents in an A and E department and more questions need to be asked about how and why the person is there. Are the injuries consistent with the story given?

4. Admissions to hospital (either frequent requests from the carer for readmission or as mentioned above admission is forced by causing a crisis due to lack of medication).

5. Falls.

6. Injuries sustained, e.g. bruises, fractures.

Indications of abuse

Every human being reacts differently to being hurt either physically or emotionally and this is certainly true of older people who have been abused. It is crucial for workers to watch for indications of abuse because, as has already been stated, physical abuse is often hidden and emotional abuse is rarely witnessed by anyone other than the victim.

In addition, to this, perhaps the most common reaction to abuse is **denial.** It is extremely hard for anyone to admit that they are being abused, especially if it is a close relative who is the abuser. The older person may be very frightened of the abuser and of the consequences if disclosure takes place. Also, an older person may be frightened of the uncertainty of the future; who else is going to look after him/her if the abuser does not? So to the victim it may seem 'safer' to remain in the abusive situation.

One indication of possible abuse is a dramatic **change in behaviour or personality,** which occurs suddenly and unexpectedly. When a person has been quite outgoing or sociable they become **withdrawn** in different ways, for example they do not want to engage in conversation, or refuse to participate in their normal activities. A quiet person may go to the opposite extreme and have **physical or verbal outbursts;** the person acts totally out of character by being unusually aggressive.

Depression or confusion may be further indications of abuse. Depression can occur gradually or very suddenly; there is no set pattern. Victims who have been sexually abused often show signs of confusion; they suddenly become confused, or existing confusion increases dramatically.

Signs of financial abuse

Trying to prove that financial abuse is perhaps taking place is one of the hardest areas of this type of work. It is only people who are involved in dealing with a person's financial affairs who are likely to pick up the fact that something is wrong, unless, of course, an older person's health is affected due to lack of food or drink. Home care staff are among the key people who may notice that an older person does not have enough to live on or that money is going missing or that arrears or debts are accruing.

Case example

Mrs B was only 60 years old and was very young looking; she had been suffering from pre-senile dementia. She could not go out alone because she got lost. Her son, S, who was 35 years old and had his own business described her as 'a **** embarrassment and wants locking up'. S used to buy things for himself using his mother's name; the bailiffs came to the house twice but the warden intervened. S also cashed his mother's pension and was supposed to pay her bills. It came to light that Mrs B had £600 rent arrears and owed £400 plus to the gas and electricity boards. The telephone was frequently disconnected and the warden used her own money to buy food for Mrs B.

Another way of finding out that someone is being financially abused is when a person repeatedly says they cannot afford something.

Case example

Eighty-four-year-old housebound Mrs J lived in a bed-sit in sheltered accommodation. She suffered from arthritis and severe depression and had attempted suicide on several occasions. She began to have regular respite care in a local authority old people's home but then said she was finding it difficult to pay for the respite stays. She had a large extended family who visited often. One particular son, L, visited more often than the others. It came to light that Mrs J gave half her pension to L to 'buy necessities' but could not tell anyone exactly what he bought for her. In fact the home help did Mrs J's shopping every week. Over the course of a few months L asked his mother to pay him £350 for emulsioning the walls of her bed-sit and then persuaded her to transfer her £1,000 savings into his name 'ready for when you go'.

Financial abuse can be done in many subtle ways. Relatives can be very persuasive and over time can convince an older person to sign over property, money etc.

Case example

Mrs V was financially abused by four members of her family; brother, sister-in-law, nephew and nephew's wife. She had a history of epileptic fits and after retiring, her nephew and his wife gave up their own house to live with her. Whilst Mrs V was in hospital she was visited by two solicitors who were sent away the first time, but on their second visit they managed to persuade Mrs V to sign a document which gave her house to her nephew and wife. The psychogeriatrician said Mrs V was lucid but when the social worker visited Mrs V did not know what she had done.

This type of abuse rarely comes to light unless the older person starts talking to someone or workers become aware that something is happening as the nursing staff did in the example above. Another indication can be when an older person is prevented from coming into care because they may have to sell their assets which others may be due to inherit in the future.

Case example

Mr and Mrs N had sold their house in Wales and moved to live in the same town as their son and daughter-in-law. Mrs N was suffering from senile dementia, was dysphasic and doubly incontinent. It was thought that Mr N was an alcoholic. He kept all the couple's money and said his wife should not have any of it. Mrs N was admitted to hospital after a fall and as her health deteriorated it was felt she needed permanent care. Mrs N's relatives refused to pay for a private nursing home.

I am sure that much abuse remains well hidden within the community and in institutions. It is no simple task to recognize it. It is rather like putting the pieces of a jigsaw together and workers must never jump to hasty conclusions.

I believe very strongly that it can take anything between two and four years to get a disclosure about abuse which has been going for a long time. It is rare that disclosure comes within days, weeks or months of working with a victim. This is why counselling for victims is so crucial; they need to know that someone who can be trusted is there to listen when the time is right.

This has implications for workers who are carrying out investigations into allegations of abuse. They may have procedures to follow, but assessments may be inconclusive because of obstacles such as denial on the part of the victim. Therefore, it is crucial that monitoring and reviewing takes place. It is important that workers keep going back if they cannot gain access. The real stumbling block is that older people are adults and if they do not want intervention there is very little professionals can do.

Nevertheless, it is important that workers improve their practice in recognizing abuse and it is hoped that the exercises in Chapter 7 may help the reader to develop skills in this area of work.

3 Working with Abuse

There are many professionals who are dealing with cases of elder abuse every day of their working lives. Some tend not to talk about it openly because this area of work is still a 'taboo subject' and is not recognized by various agencies. Consequently, not many professional people know who is doing what. It is only when a group of people come together and share experiences that we learn how the various professionals are working with older victims in different work settings and out in the community.

There is a definite need to raise consciousness that elder abuse is an important issue. The problem of abused older people is likely to increase in the future as there are going to be more older people in the population than ever before. It is predicted that by the end of this century one third of the population will be over retirement age. The agencies involved in working with older people are going to have to give recognition to this fact and plan resources appropriately.

During the course of my research I found that once professionals started thinking about abuse they actually started to recognize it; 'I never thought about it before until you started going on about it. Now I've realized Mrs X has been financially abused for years and I'd not cottoned on' (social worker).

In a different setting I was told by a consultant that his hospital had had no more than three cases of abuse in the past ten years. He then referred seven cases to me in the next nine months. When teaching workshops on elder abuse I have found people start to think about past cases they have been involved with and suddenly realize they have 'missed' a case of abuse or they admit they 'did nothing' because they did not know what to do.

Simple rules in working with abuse

1. Workers, whatever their role, must listen to older people.

It is easy to dismiss what an older person says because they may present as being forgetful, confused, unreliable etc. Even if the person is suffering from senile dementia, whatever is said must be given due consideration. It seems that there is usually some grain of truth in a dementing person's rambling, even if it relates back to something which happened many years ago.

Case example

Eighty-year-old Mrs K kept referring to the fact that she had been raped. Nobody took much notice of her because she was starting to dement. The support worker eventually met other members of the family who were able to explain that Mrs K and her sisters had been sexually abused by their brother when they had been teenagers.

There could also be some truth in what is being said about the present; workers should never dismiss what is said to them. At the same time, it is sometimes necessary to look beyond what is being said. All too often a victim continually denies what is happening and emphasizes 'everything is fine' when in fact it is the complete opposite.

Another indication that something may be wrong is when an older person seems to be a 'nuisance' because they are always asking for some form of help, for example requesting daily visits from the general practitioner, asking the home help to call in more often or do one more trip to the shops. This may be a genuine plea for help in an indirect way.

2. Abuse cannot be ignored.

It is all too easy to ignore a case of elder abuse, especially if the victim denies what is happening and refuses all help. Both morally and professionally, workers should not ignore such cases.

Even when confronted with denial a worker should continue to offer the victim the opportunity to talk about what is happening. It may take years to build up enough trust for a person to admit what is happening to them. Once disclosure has taken place, careful consideration must be given to how to proceed with the information. Here we return to the theme of the professional dilemma—**Do Wo Do Something or Leave Things As They Are?** Sometimes a person may be more at risk if action is taken; the abuser is confronted by the social worker, police or someone similar and then nothing comes of the investigation. Workers should be aware of outcomes and, if they are not able to give regular support to a victim, safety measures should be taken, for example by informing the warden or home help of the situation and asking them to monitor closely the older person and abuser. If a social worker is not already involved, it may be appropriate to inform a duty social worker or the principal social worker for that particular area and explain that the older person may now be more at risk.

What is crucial is that help has to be offered to the victim after disclosure has taken place. Just because a person is old does not mean that therapy is of no value. It could be particularly beneficial to older women who have been sexually abused. As in cases of child abuse, they need to talk about what has happened to them and they need ongoing support. It should not be bottled up because other people cannot face what has happened.

Help should also be offered to the abuser. In the case of the carer who abuses it may come as a great relief to be able to talk openly about the stress which he or she has been under. Or, if the abuser has a specific problem, some specialist help may be offered.

Case example

Mrs T was in her seventies and had always had a close relationship with her grandson. When Mrs T's daughter remarried, the grandson came to live with her. She then sold her house and spent money 'living it up' with her grandson. When all the money had gone they presented themselves as homeless and were rehoused by the local authority. Mrs T then developed arthritis and could not go out much. The grandson, aged 21, had a lot of personal problems and was not a sociable person. He was very overweight and was depressed, not only by this problem but also by the lack of a job and money. The social worker believed the abuse was related to money as he wanted his grandmother's pension for himself. Mrs T took out an injunction so that her grandson could no longer live with her. The social worker helped the grandson find alternative accommodation and worked with him on his specific personal problems.

The multi-disciplinary approach

At present many professionals are working in isolation with cases of elder abuse. The way forward must be to adopt the multi-disciplinary approach so that information is shared regularly, clear objectives are set, there is co-ordination of services, decisions are made and workers can support each other as well as the older person with whom they are working.

A wide range of people could be involved with an older person:

Home help
Warden
Social worker
Day care staff
Care staff—local authority
           —private
General practitioner
Consultant
Hospital nursing staff
Community psychiatric nurse

District nurse
Health Visitor
Occupational therapist
Physiotherapist
Speech therapist
Professional carer
Housing officer
Volunteer

There are many roles and tasks to be performed when working with cases of elder abuse. Three basic concepts are crucial for good practice:

- Building trust
- Being honest
- Respecting confidentiality

It has already been acknowledged that it may be extremely difficult for a person to talk about the abuse which they are suffering, especially if the abuser is a close relative. Putting trust in an outsider can be difficult and may take time to develop. It also takes a lot of confidence to disclose about abuse and so it is thus important for professionals to try to make the person feel safe enough and confident enough to disclose.

Professionals must be honest at all times both with clients and colleagues. An older person is more likely to confide in you if he or she knows you have been honest. The older person also needs to know that everything they say is in the utmost confidence and that, if they do not want any action to be taken, this will be respected (no matter how frustrating it is for the professional to whom they have confided).

In such situations sometimes the only thing a professional can do is to listen, but it is important that the older person is made aware of what options may be available both for a victim and abuser. The choice to accept or reject help is then the victim's but the professional should be there to support and help in making that decision. The case of Mr P who was abused by four youths was mentioned in a previous chapter. The four youths were eventually prosecuted by the police but since then Mr P has been abused by other people in the community. He is vulnerable because he has learning difficulties and is a well known character in the community. But how can he be protected adequately? After the last attack he was discharged from hospital to an old people's home for a short stay. He quickly became institutionalized and was losing his independence. It was felt a transfer to a sheltered housing complex would be a safer environment for Mr P because he could be well supported by the home care staff and the day centre in the local old people's home which is located nearby. However Mr P wished to return to his own home where he had lived with his mother until she died 16 years previously and where he is probably very much at risk of being attacked again in the community.

There can be different stages in working with elder abuse:

- Assessment
- Planning
- Intervention
- Monitoring
- Reviewing

There may not be a particular order to these stages because it will depend on each individual case which presents itself. If there is a crisis there may not be time to do extensive planning. However if suspicions are aroused over time about the welfare of an older person, a full assessment may be carried out and a decision taken to monitor the situation in order to gain more information for the future.

It is important that *everyone* communicates because the various professionals often hold different bits of information. Professionals who currently work alone may find this approach difficult to adopt at first as there may be some feelings of mistrust between professionals and their agencies. Sometimes there is a lack of understanding between professionals about their roles and procedures in different agencies. District nurses have frequently commented to me that it is 'useless referring an older person to social services because nothing gets done'. Priorities can be different in agencies and this can cause conflict and mistrust.

Assessment

People who are abused are not always going to appear conveniently in the casualty department of a local hospital or be a client of the social services department. Abuse can be ongoing for years without anyone realizing that it is taking place. Therefore, anyone who is involved with an older person needs to be aware of the indicators of abuse (see Chapter 2). Full and proper assessments need to be carried out in whichever setting one is working. Professionals need to take time to find out the necessary information and to compile a social history.

Monitoring

Professionals often suspect that an older person is being abused but find it difficult to prove. It is important to keep monitoring situations and not to give up. A key worker needs to be designated so that all information can be collated. This person does not have to be a social worker; other people may be visiting more frequently and be more likely to gain the trust and confidence of the older person. For example, a home help may be dealing with an older person's finances and will notice if money is missing. As has been said previously, one of the problems in dealing with cases where physical abuse is suspected lies in identifying the nature of the injuries. Injuries are rarely visible as they are commonly inflicted on parts of the body which remain hidden and not many people actually see an older person's body. An exception may be the district nurse who baths older people regularly or the warden who dresses and undresses the older person. But older people cannot be monitored as easily as children, who are seen regularly by health visitors in their early years and who can be monitored carefully by nurseries and schools.

Reviewing

Again, because older people are not considered to be a priority, cases can be left to drift, especially if no dramatic events are reported. In cases of elder abuse professionals should be arguing that cases should continue to be monitored and reviewed regularly. It is important to review abuse cases at *regular* intervals in case any information has been missed or not communicated to the key worker. Professionals often make the comment that little can be done to protect an abused older person. However, it seems clear that an older person can be protected if ongoing support is given.

Case example

Mr and Mrs H were refusing all help and Mrs H was reluctant to talk about her husband's violence. The social work assistant continued to visit on a weekly basis in order to support the couple. Eventually they did accept some practical help and a support package was designed for them which offered four days at a local day centre and respite care for Mr H in a local authority old people's home. Mrs H also disclosed her husband's violence to the social work assistant and home care organizer two years later. As a result of relieving some of the stress on Mrs H her family, who had refused to visit or have anything to do with her, actually came back together and were very supportive towards her. This may not have happened had the social work assistant closed the case two years previously.

The case conference

Some professionals have a horror of case conferences concerning elder abuse because of bad experiences when working with child abuse cases. I have heard it said that we 'should not be going down the same road as child abuse'. I have also heard people thrash out the use of words—should it be a case conference, or case discussion or perhaps a case meeting? We all have our own preferences. For the purpose of this book I shall use the term *case conference*, by which I mean a forum where people can share information.

There can be a number of reasons why it would be beneficial to convene a case conference. Obviously, if a person is abused or if there are concerns that a person may be at risk, a conference is needed to assess the situation and to plan future intervention, support, monitoring and reviewing. This would normally be accepted as good practice. Professionals need to be clear about the purpose of convening a case conference and consequently guidelines must address this issue and state clearly both the purpose and tasks of a case conference. The main purposes are to:

- share information in a multidisciplinary forum
- assess the older person's situation and the degree of risk
- make decisions and recommendations.

This all sounds fine in theory, but professionals must get better at putting the theory into practice. There has to be commitment from *all* professionals to work in a multidisciplinary way, which means giving some commitment to attending an elder abuse case conference. If someone cannot attend, then a written report should be available for the conference. It is pointless bringing professionals together if all the relevant information is not readily available.

Case conferences can offer support and focus to a worker. It is the opportunity to vent concerns, but also to plan some constructive ways of working. Elder abuse is a difficult and demanding area of work; cases are often very complex. Workers may be facing dilemmas and need support. The case conference can be used to express doubts, anxieties and uncertainties. A professional may gain information, insight and support from other professionals which will help them in the future. Basically, it is a way of giving some structure and framework to working with elder abuse, where previously cases of elder abuse may have been left to drift.

There are too many cliches around like 'we'll monitor the situation', 'we'll review in the future', 'convene when appropriate'; all this can give way to bad practice. Workers must become more concise, by preparing for a case conference. They need to do this with the help of their line managers. Some questions to be considered in preparing for a case conference are listed in Figure 3.1.

Who should be invited to the case conference?

When is it? (Check date and time)

Where? (Check venue)

Who will take the minutes?

Are any special facilities/arrangements needed? (e.g. interpreter, someone to sign, access for wheelchair, a separate room in case victim and abuser have to be kept away from each other)

What information is needed?

What do I know?

What more do I need to know?

Is the file record up to date?

What do I want to say?

Whose views am I representing? (my own, the agency, the client?)

What should I put on a list of key points?

Have I completed all the necessary forms?

What are my true feelings about this case?

Figure 3.1 Preparing for a Case Conference – questions to ask yourself

'At risk' registers

There is also resistance to the thought of 'at risk' registers, but again, they could have some value. Registers could be held by the local authority or health authority. Local agencies, when forming multidisciplinary guidelines and procedures, must be clear about why they want to have a register and then formulate clear criteria for such a register.

Solihull Joint Consultative Committee in 'Guidelines for managing suspected abuse of vulnerable adults' states the registration criteria as follows:

1. Any vulnerable person who it is reasonable to believe meets one or more of the definitions of vulnerable adult abuse used within these procedures AND where there is an agreed need for a protection plan to ensure the safety and welfare of that adult should have their name placed on the Register.

2. Where a vulnerable adult, known to have been registered in another area moves to Solihull the person's name will immediately be included on the register on a temporary basis by a Team Manager pending the calling of an initial case conference. (Solihull 1994, p.22)

A register held by a health authority could be a way of monitoring risk. It is worrying that, although many abused older people may present in Casualty Departments at regular intervals, the frequency of their visits is not picked up. A register could record the number of referrals, falls, bruises, other injuries and so forth. In some health authorities, older people who present at night in Casualty Departments are automatically followed up at home within two to six working days by a district nurse.

Procedures and guidelines

The value of having procedures and guidelines was discussed in Chapter 1. It is important that if guidelines exist they should state clearly what procedures should be followed. For example, for case conferences it is important to address such issues as:

- When should conferences be convened?
- Who attends (are the victim/carer/advocate invited?)
- Who chairs/sets the agenda/minutes?

If an 'at risk' register is to exist, its purpose needs to be stated and criteria for inclusion on the register clearly defined. Other issues to be addressed are:

- What information is included on the register?
- Who has access to the information?
- Who takes the decision about registration?
- Who informs the older person?
- Should a system of complaints be instigated?

I think it is also crucial that guidelines state what outcomes are expected from a case conference. This is because historically much work with older people has been very informal. If a person is at risk of abuse some formal way of working to monitor the situation needs to be implemented. This is the value of formulating a protection plan during the case conference. The plan gives everyone something to work with. Points which need to be considered are:

- **Who will be the keyworker?** (to co-ordinate information and ensure implementation of the plan)
- **Will there be a primary worker?** (someone who has more face to face contact with the victim)
- **Who will do what and when?** (the plan needs to state clearly roles, responsibilities, specific tasks of each person involved; it is no good saying Ms X will visit regularly – what does 'regularly' mean?)
- **When will the case be reviewed/case conference reconvened?**

Obviously, the plan will not work if the older person is not in agreement. If the victim is not present at the case conference, then s/he must be consulted about the plan immediately after the case conference.

The law

One of the most frustrating things in working with elder abuse is the fact that there is little legislation to protect vulnerable older people. At present it is not possible to take out any sort of Place of Safety Order when there are suspicions that a person is being abused. The law assumes that adults are responsible for their own actions. If a person is willing to make a complaint to the police or there has been a witness to a crime, the abuser can then be charged although for many reasons victims are likely to be unwilling to press charges. The following list shows offences with which some abusers could be charged:

Murder

Attempted murder

Manslaughter

Section 18 wounding

Section 20 wounding

Section 47 assault

Rape

Attempted rape

Indecent assault—female

Indecent assault—male

Theft

Another option is for the victim to take out an injunction to prevent the abuser coming in the vicinity. Again, it is the responsibility of professionals to ensure that the victim is aware of their rights and of what could be done. But it is also important to be honest about what taking proceedings may entail—for example having to give evidence in a court of law.

But what about older people who are not mentally sound and cannot protect themselves? Section 47 of the National Assistance Act (1948) enables a local authority to make an application to a magistrates court to remove a person from his home on the grounds:

1. That the person is suffering from grave chronic disease or being aged or infirm or physically incapacitated, is living in insanitary conditions.

2. That the person is unable to devote to himself and is not receiving from other persons proper care and attention.

3. That his removal from home is necessary either in his own interests or for preventing injury to the health of, or serious nuisance to other persons.

Section 47 is very rarely used as community physicians are often reluctant to give their support to the application. The Law Commission has been working in recent years on ways of working with mentally incapacitated and other vulnerable adults (Law Commission 1991, 1993a,1993b,1993c,):

'Section 47 of the National Assistance Act 1948 and the National Assistance (Amendment) Act 1951 should be repealed and replaced by a new scheme giving clearer and more appropriate powers to local social services authorities to intervene to protect incapacitated, mentally disordered or vulnerable people.' (Law Commission 1993c Section 2.10 pp.15–16)

Paper 130 proposes the use of entry warrants, examination and assessment orders and emergency protection orders. Other legislation is given consideration, for example Guardianship Orders under the Mental Health Act. Applying for guardianship involves a lot of paper work and is time consuming for legislation which currently has many loopholes. There are three basic powers under these orders:

1. To say where someone is to live.
2. To require a person to attend for medical treatment, occupation, education or training.
3. To require access to the patient to be given to doctors, approved social workers or other persons specified by the guardian.

Currently, sections 115, 135 and 136 of the Mental Health Act 1983 are used in some cases of elder abuse. Section 115 is about powers of entry and inspection. An approved social worker can enter and inspect any premises in which a mentally disordered person is living if there is reasonable cause to believe the person is not receiving proper care.

Under Section 135 a person can be detained for 72 hours. The criterion is:

'There is reasonable cause to suspect that a person believed to be suffering from mental disorder has been (a) ill-treated or neglected or not kept under proper control, or is (b) unable to care for himself and is living alone.' (Gostin 1983 p.19)

Under Section 136:

'It appears to a police officer that a person in a public place is 'suffering from mental disorder' and is in immediate need of care or control' (Gostin *ibid.* p.18)

The person can be taken to a place of safety and examined by a medical practitioner and interviewed by an approved social worker.

Although financial abuse is often subtly carried out and in fact often remains well hidden, there are some positive ways to deal with it. Much will depend on whether the victim is mentally alert and whether they actually want any intervention to stop the abuse.

It has been said earlier that one of the most common forms of financial abuse is when someone is cashing a pension and then not handing the money over or is taking a large part of it. The victim may wish to authorize someone else to cash their pension by signing the back of their pension book, therefore making that person an *agent*. Another option is to make someone (relative, friend, professional) an *appointee* by applying to the Department of Social Security. If it is actually the appointee who is abusing the older person, this can be reported to the Department of Social Security and the matter will be investigated. However, this can only be done with the consent of the victim.

Financial abuse is particularly common when someone is admitted to hospital and remains there for sometime. The pension book can 'disappear' and the victim is left short of money.

Case example

Mrs E's only daughter died suddenly 15 years ago and Mrs E had never come to terms with this. The only link left with her daughter was her son-in-law, B, who financially abused her. At 85 years of age Mrs E was suffering from angina and heart failure. She was forgetful but not dementing. When Mrs E came into hospital she did not have any money and her pension book was missing. It came to light that B was always telling Mrs E she owed money and consequently she handed money over to him. Whilst in hospital B had the missing pension book and cashed over £300. He still told Mrs E she owed money even though the social worker had used trust funds to pay off arrears.

If a pension book is missing it is possible to ask the Department of Social Security to put a stop on the book. A new book will be issued. Again, the consent of the victim is needed for this procedure.

When an older person has substantial assets, it is possible to approach the Court of Protection for help in order to protect and help manage their financial affairs. The Court of Protection is:

...an office of the Supreme Court. Its function is to manage and administer the property and affairs of people who, through mental disorder, are incapable of managing their own financial affairs. The Court draws its powers from the Mental Health Act 1983 and the Court of Protection Rules 1984. 'Patient' is the name given by the act to a person who is suffering from mental disorder and whose financial affairs are subject to the Court's control . . . A receiver is a person appointed by the Court to deal with the day to day management of the patient's financial affairs. He or she can be a relative, a friend, an official of the local authority or perhaps a professional advisor. If there is no-one else suitable or willing to act, the public trustee can be appointed in the last resort. (Public Trust Office, April 1988, p.1)

An Enduring Power of Attorney enables people, while they are still mentally capable, to decide who they would like to deal with their affairs for them even after they become mentally incapable. An Enduring Power of Attorney is:

...a Power of Attorney which, subject to conditions and safeguards, continues in force even after the maker of the power (called 'the Donor') becomes mentally incapable of handling his or her affairs, provided that it is registered... An Attorney is someone who can act on behalf of a Donor in financial matters. If the Donor gives the Attorney(s) general authority to act on her or his behalf in relation to all the Donor's business matters the Attorney(s) will be able to do almost anything that the Donor could have done, for example, sign cheques, withdraw money from savings accounts, buy or sell shares or buy or sell houses. (Public Trust Office, July 1990, p.3–5)

What resources are used now

A major issue in working with cases of elder abuse is to consider what resources are appropriate to help both the victim and the abuser. Social workers intervene in many different ways indicating commitment and imagination but the lack of agreed procedures. In many cases social workers may try to remove the victim from the abusive situation. However, it could be argued that it is wrong to remove the victim from his/her home where s/he may have lived for many years. It may be more appropriate to offer resources to the abuser. This is especially true when it is the abuser who has specific problems, for example suffering from senile dementia. The following resources may be used for either a victim or abuser:

1. Day care—either in a local authority day centre or a health authority day hospital.
2. Night care—in the same settings as above.
3. Short-term care.
4. Respite care—this provides regular short stays either in a local authority home, private care or in a hospital. Length of respite stays can vary considerably from two weeks in, six weeks out; one month in, or one month out etc.
5. Permanent care—either local authority provision or in the private sector.

Resources 1 to 4 can be particularly helpful in relieving stress in many situations. If a carer is reaching the end of his or her tether, a few hours relief may help them to carry on for a little longer. Night care has found to be very useful for older people who are suffering from senile dementia and do not sleep at night. If they attend a night centre this enables the carer to have a proper night's sleep. Resources can be used in various ways; sometimes a couple may wish to attend the day centre or they may attend different centres to get a break from each other.

Case example

Mrs C suffered from severe senile dementia but physically she was fit and strong. For 13 years she had been cared for by her frail husband who was suffering from cancer. MrC never asked for any help until his daughter visited from Australia and was shocked at what her father was having to do. When the social services department became involved, initially Mrs C was offered five days at a day centre in a home for the elderly mentally infirm and soon after she was offered respite care in the same home. Mr C missed his wife during the day and even more so when she went in for respite care and eventually permanent care. Mr C was abused physically and financially by his son. As he was mentally alert it was arranged that he went to a local day centre once a week and occasionally he had short-term care until his health deteriorated to such a degree that he was admitted into permanent care.

What resources should be used in the future

In the above section I have discussed the resources which are most commonly used in cases of elder abuse and I am aware that workers use a variety of other resources to help victims and abusers. During the course of my research I have asked professionals and clients about what resources are needed to work with abused older people and the abusers.

1. What the workers say

A common response from professionals is 'we need more resources' in the form of day care, short-term care, respite care and there is a general feeling of frustration that in the present climate of financial uncertainty additional resources cannot be obtained. Yet as more older people remain in the community there is likely to be an increase in demand for such resources.

Professionals need to respond quickly to crisis situations and therefore emergency beds need to be made available either in local authority homes or hospital so that a victim has a safe place to go. Family placement schemes can also offer a safe environment. Older people can be cared for by going to stay with a family who have been trained to care for older people. This resource can be used in a crisis or as an ongoing resource, either for the victim or the abuser.

More resources need to be put into the home. As well as increasing services such as home help, warden, district nurses, community psychiatric nurses, and more resources from the voluntary sector or homemakers should be made available. Carers who are feeling isolated need more practical help, for example having sitters so that they themselves can go out and have some social life. Many voluntary agencies are now organising sitting services for people in their local communities.

Often older people become more confused and disorientated when moved to a new environment for care, so workers who have homemakers find this resource more beneficial. A homemaker can go to 'live in' up to 14 working days (they usually work in pairs to cover each other) with the older person. S/he can do the practical tasks such as shopping, cooking, cleaning but also can engage in counselling and therapy. Whilst supporting someone in their home, the homemaker can also monitor what is happening. For example, if a victim is living with an abuser, the homemaker may witness what triggers off an abusive incident. Again it is important to state that homemakers can work with the victim *and* abuser.

2. What the victims say

Some victims I have interviewed have been very clear about what they would have liked in order to help them. One woman who was physically abused by her husband said that she would like the chance to go to a refuge '...but not all women. I don't hate men. There should be places for old people like me, men and women, where we can go and feel safe. In 64 years I've never had anywhere to run to'.

The victims who did not actually want to leave home said that at times they wanted to talk anonymously to someone and felt that a Helpline would have been therapeutic for them. There was quite a lot of resentment towards Childline, because many victims felt that children got all the attention from the media and older people were always left out or lumped with something else—'I was told I could ring the Samaritans'.

Others wanted to talk face-to-face with someone but not in their own homes. They found it useful that they could talk to staff in day hospitals, day centres, residential units. Many victims wanted someone to talk on their behalf, but not a social worker. The victim often said they felt 'nervous' or inadequate. The use of advocates is imperative in these situations, but also in cases where abuse takes place in an institution. Victims may feel that they cannot say what is happening because staff will 'take it out on me' or the social worker may collude with the residential staff because 'they all work for the same place'.

3. The reality

Although we are supposed to be working in a needs-led way, the reality today is that social workers are doing full needs assessments and then they are not able to provide the resources. This is because we are constantly working in a climate of economic restraint. Social workers are always saying to me 'all we do is full needs assessments. We don't do proper social work anymore'.

One of the most vital resources in working with abuse is the 'listening ear'. Because the majority of victims do not want to leave the abusive situation it is often not possible to offer practical resources. Proper counselling and therapy is needed for both victims and abusers. I believe in many cases it can take years to get a disclosure, not weeks or months. With shortages of staff, are these cases going to be kept open? I doubt it.

Therefore, the services of specialist workers, that is, counsellors and therapists will have to be bought in. Social services departments are going to have use Community Care budgets to purchase people who can provide extra help to work with elder abuse.

Where do we go from here?

People who are working with older people must not assume that nothing can be achieved in an abusive situation. It is necessary to believe that there can be a positive outcome. Working with older people is often a low priority in many agencies. Professionals who are committed to working with older people are aware of the increasing problems of elder abuse. As a summary, the following issues need to be considered and discussed in order to increase awareness amongst all professionals:

1. Recognition that there is a problem regarding elder abuse.
2. Procedures and guidelines.
3. Support from the agency and line managers.
4. Training for people working with abused older people—to help with the assessment of risk, identification and intervention.
5. Resources—services must be geared to the needs of older people.
6. Crisis and emergency services should be made readily available.
7. Support services to alleviate long-term stress and also facilitate monitoring.
8. Case planning, monitoring and reviewing.

9. Liaison between professionals, working in multi-disciplinary teams, co-ordination of services between agencies.

10. Race and culture—considering abuse which takes place in ethnic minorities, how this can be monitored and ascertaining the needs of the abused older people, and the abusers.

4 Some Basic Facts

It is not the purpose of this book to go into detail about the research which has been carried out in the United Kingdom and the United States of America during recent years. At the end of the book I have suggested reading material to facilitate futher learning. However, it may be useful to have some very basic facts which will make the subject of elder abuse more comprehensible. The objective of this chapter is to summarize some of the findings which have come out of a research study which has been undertaken in Sheffield over a three year period.

A brief history

Research into abuse of older people has been very limited within the United Kingdom. In the early 1980s the term 'granny bashing' was bandied about and papers about the subject started to appear. In 1984 Mervyn Eastman published 'Old Age Abuse' which was a major contribution to the subject area and he has continued to write about the problem (Eastman 1994). In 1984 he could cite two major studies on old age abuse which had been carried out in this country, namely Dr. Elizabeth Hocking's study in Swindon (1972 to 1982) and the Community Care Survey (1983). Few detailed studies have been carried out since then but during the past few years there has been an upsurge in interest and individuals are carrying out their own research in different settings. As yet there is no central agency that can inform us about who is doing what.

Research in Sheffield

I had had several proven cases of elder abuse on my caseload while working as a social worker for the Sheffield Family and Community Services Department. During the six years I worked in an area office I became increasingly aware that other workers were coming across cases of abuse more frequently. I started to question not only what I was doing with my abuse cases but also what other social workers were doing when faced with an abused older person. Consequently, in 1988 I decided to carry out a small study in order to find out how many cases of elder abuse had been identified in my area office during the previous twelve month period. The study continued for a second year during 1989 and then during 1990 expanded to cover two other area offices plus a social work department within a hospital. In total, 65 cases were monitored. Social workers, social work assistants and home care staff were asked to contact me if they came across a case of elder abuse so that I could conduct individual interviews with them. An interview schedule was designed to ask about the victims, the abusers, the injuries sustained, intervention and procedures used and final outcomes.

The victims

The abused older person has tended to be stereotyped as follows: 'the majority are female, over 80 and are dependant as a result of physical or mental incapacity' (Eastman 1984, p.41). In Sheffield 48 (74%) of the victims were female and 17 (26%) were male. The ages ranged from 60 to 98 years old the average age being 64 years. The majority were *not* over 80 years old, as Table 4.1 shows.

The interviewees were asked about the characteristics of the victims. It should not be assumed that victims are dependent either mentally or physically. Very often they can be mentally sound but have some physical or medical problem. Table 4.2

Table 4.1 Ages of victims

Age	No.	%
60–69	14	21
70–79	24	37
80–89	22	34
90 +	5	8
Total	65	100

Table 4.2 Victims: Types of personal, physical and medical problems experienced

Agoraphobia	Heart trouble
Alcoholism	High blood pressure
Amputation	Incontinence
Anaemia	Learning disability
Angina	Left hemiparesis
Arthritis	Leg ulcers
Blindness	Leukemia
Bowel problem	Liver problems
Brain damage	Mentally handicapped
Damaged spine	Overweight
Deafness	Parkinson's disease
Depression	Partially sighted
Diabetes	Pernicious anaemia
Diverticular disease	Physical handicap
Dysphasia	Prostate problems
Eczema	Psychiatric problems
Epilepsy	Senile dementia
Forgetful	Speech limited
Frailty	Stomach complaint
Glaucoma	Stroke

summarizes the personal, medical or physical problems which some of the victims suffered. The problems listed are direct quotes from the interviewees.

The abusers

'The abuser is typically identified as being female, middle aged and usually the offspring of the abused' (p 104 Gelles and Cornell (1985).

The findings in Sheffield do not support this stereotype picture of the abuser. The majority of abusers were male. The ages ranged from 11 to 89 years old. It is difficult to give an exact number of abusers because in some cases victims were abused by more than one person and in several cases victims were abused by gangs of school children or youths living in the local community. Interviewees could therefore on occasions not give definite information about the abusers. However, information was obtained about 70 abusers, 44 (63%) of whom were male and 26 (37%) were female. It was noted that all members of the gangs of youths who abused older people were male. There were no reports of any female youths being involved.

Table 4.3 Age of abusers

Age	No.	%
10–19	1	1.5
20–29	2	3
30–39	14	20.5
40–49	10	15
50–59	9	13
60–69	11	16
70–79	9	13
80–89	12	18
90 +	-	-
Total	**68**	**100**

Although 70 abusers were identified, it was not always possible to get additional information about such matters as age, personal characteristics, specific problems etc. Table 4.3 shows the details obtained regarding age of abusers.

Thirty-nine (60%) of the victims actually lived with the person who abused them. The abusers were not always blood related to the victim. Table 4.4 illustrates the relationship the abuser had with the victim.

Table 4.4 Relationship between victim and abuser

Abused by	No. of victims
Wife	5
Husband	16
Son	15
Daughter	9
Son-in-law	4
Daughter-in-law	3
Grandson	3
Granddaughter	2
Brother	1
Nephew	1
Nephew's wife	1
General practitioner	1
Neighbour	2
Men living in same household	1
Gangs of youths	7
Friend	2

Interviewees were asked about the known characteristics of the abusers. The majority (with the exclusion of the school children) spent most of their time in the home rather than at work, as shown in Table 4.5.

Table 4.5 Occupation of abuser

Occupation	No.
Schoolchild	Exact no. not known
Employed	15
Unemployed	21
Long term sick	1
Retired	29

Table 4.6 Abusers: types of personal, physical and medical problems experienced

Alcoholism	Mentally unbalanced
Anxiety neurosis	Paget's disease
Arthritis	Paranoia
Blindness	Parkinson's disease
Cancer	Physical handicap
Confusion	Psychiatric problems
Depression	Recurring mental breakdowns
Epilepsy	Schizophrenia
Financial	Stroke
Gynaecological problems	Violence
Learning disability	Weight problem
Mental illness	Withered arm

Table 4.6 illustrates the types of problem experienced by abusers. Again the terminology regarding personal, medical and physical problems are direct quotes from the interviewees.

Type of abuse which took place

I stated in Chapter 1 that it is difficult to define abuse, as we all have different values and attitudes. Researchers also experience problems when trying to categorize cases of elder abuse. Cases are often complex and in many situations victims experience more than one type of abuse. This was found to be true in Sheffield where victims experienced physical abuse (44) emotional abuse (17) and financial abuse (34).

The injuries

One of the problems in dealing with cases where abuse is suspected lies in identifying the nature of the injuries. Older people bruise very easily and the injuries are often thought to have been caused by falling. When I conducted the interviews, few of the interviewees had actually seen definite injuries and the information regarding the actual injuries tended to be vague rather than specific:

'various lumps and bruises'

'injury to the nose'

'covered in scratches all over'

When dealing with cases of child abuse, social workers are much more specific about injuries, aware that they must be able to describe the injuries and their location on the body. In cases of elder abuse, the worker is unlikely to have to produce such evidence in a court of law. Furthermore, it is extremely difficult (and probably inappropriate) for a worker to ask an older person to remove clothes in order to look at suspected injuries. Table 4.7 lists the types of injuries mentioned.

Table 4.7 Types of injuries mentioned

Bruising	Cracked ribs
Burns	Fractures
Cigarette burns	Lacerations
Cuts	

The injuries had been inflicted by hitting with hands/fists, kicking, slapping, shaking, pushing or elbowing. Some interviewees could say where the injuries had occurred on the body either because they had seen the injuries themselves or because they had received such information from another source (see Tables 4.8 and 4.9).

Table 4.8 Injuries: location on body

Arms	Jaw
Eyes	Legs
Face	Thigh
Forehead	Wrist
Head	Back

Table 4.9 Who saw the injuries

Day centre staff	2
District nurse	3
Home care organizer	2
Warden/home help	9
Hospital staff	4
General practitioner	3
Neighbour	4
Relative	4

Hearing about the abuse

Interviewees were asked how they had learnt about the abuse of their clients. Their sources are listed in Table 4.10.

Social workers seemed to accept information that an older person had injuries and did not routinely examine the injuries for themselves. Again, if these had been cases of child abuse I

Table 4.10 Hearing about abuse: sources

Sources	No.
Abuser	1
Case file	1
Consultant	1
Day centre staff	2
District nurse	3
Family aides	1
General practitioner	3
Home help/warden	25
Home care organizer	8
Hospital staff	7
Neighbour	5
Relative	3
Victim	11

suggest that more precise procedures would have been available and followed. For example, a child would be taken to a hospital in order to ascertain how the injuries had been incurred. In some cases the older person was admitted to hospital by the general practitioner, but only in a few cases were the causes of the injuries fully investigated.

Frequency of abuse

Interviewees were asked whether they thought the abuse was ongoing or a one-off incident. In 62 (95%) of the cases it was thought that the abuse was ongoing. Most interviewees could not be precise about how long the abuse had been occurring or pinpoint a time when it had started. Some felt it may have only been a few months, others estimated that the abuse had been going on for as long as 15 years while others were aware that marital violence had been occurring throughout certain marriages which could be as long as over 60 years.

Intervention and outcome

Interviewees were asked what happened once they knew or suspected their clients had been abused. They were asked about who became involved and what they, personally, did. The social workers actually intervened in many different ways, indicating commitment and imagination but the lack of agreed procedures. When I asked social workers about the procedures they themselves had followed, the majority said that they had been unsure about what to do. By contrast, if these had been cases of child abuse they would have known exactly what to do. Few workers actually convened case conferences or case discussions. General practice seemed to involve liaison with a range of people, for example general practitioners, home helps, day centre staff in order to share information. However, there was often a lack of co-ordination and no systematic procedures for monitoring or reviewing situations.

Resources can be used both for the victim and abuser. Many workers would argue that a victim should not be the person who should be removed from the violent environment—rather, it should be the abuser. Again, similar arguments have been made when working with child abuse. Some workers developed packages of care for both the victim and abuser. Table 4.11 shows a summary of resources and facilities used to help both victims and abusers.

Table 4.11 Summary of resources used for victims and abusers

Local Authority

Day centre	17
Short-term care	11
Respite care	7
Permanent Part III	4
Emergency bed	2
Family placement scheme	2

Table 4.11 Summary of resources used
for victims and abusers (continued)

Hospital

Emergency admission	3
Respite care	7
Day hospital	3

Other

Day centre for the blind	1
Luncheon club	4
Meals-on-wheels	4
Housing department	
—sheltered accommodation	1
—rehousing offer	1
Private nursing home	4
Warden/home help	38
District nurse	13
Community psychiatric nurse	4
Physiotherapist	2
Speech therapist	1

5 What it's Like to be Abused

It is all very well talking about abuse—what it is, how do we recognize it and how do we work with it—but how many of us really know how it feels to be abused when you are an older person?

I felt it was important to get the victim's point of view. The following pages contain parts of a dialogue which took place between a victim (V) and an interviewer (I).

The victim agreed to talk about the abuse she had experienced three years previously. She was financially abused by her daughter and physically abused by her son-in-law. She was aged 64 years and in poor health. She suffered from emphysema, heart trouble, gynaecological problems, severe arthritis and rheumatism. The family structure was as follows:

Daughter: Cath (abuser)—age 32

Son-in-law: Gary (abuser)—age 31

Grandchildren: Thomas—age 11
                          Lee—age 9

Daughter: Gail

Son: Paul

I.   I understand that you've been a resident here for quite sometime. How long have you actually lived here?

V.   Nearly two and a half years.

I.   And where were you living before?

V.   At N _____ .

I.   Did you live on your own?

V.   Yes.

I.   In what sort of accommodation?

V.   Two bedroomed flat.

I.   And why did you actually come to live in an old people's home?

V.   Because my daughter was asking me for money all the time and it just got me down. I couldn't stand it no more.

I.   How long had this been going on?

V.   Well to tell you the truth, when she was out in Germany she wrote to ask me for a lot of money and I sent it to her and I never got it back.

I.   What sort of sums of money are we talking about?

V.   About £400.

I.   Did she ever give a reason what she wanted the money for?

V.   Well she said she wanted it for her husband because he had gone and got a car out there and the fellow had threatened him.

I.   And when you were living at N _____ . how often did she ask you for money then?

V.   About nearly every week.

I.   And how much did she actually take from you?

V.   Sometimes she would take £5 or £10, sometimes more.

I.   Did she promise to pay you back or did she just take it?

V.   Well she said she would give it me back but I've never had it back.

I.   Did you find that you were getting into debt yourself?

V.   Yes.

I.   What sort of debts did you have?

V.   I had the gas and the electricity which they came to
     threaten me to cut it off and I had to ask for help then.

I.   And how much did you actually owe on those bills?

V.   About £300 on one and £200 on the other, something like
     that.

I.   Did you get behind in your rent as well?

V.   Yes.

I.   And did your daughter talk to you about this?

V.   Well I told her about it but she just didn't let it seem to
     bother her.

I.   I believe there was an incident with your pension book
     before you gave up your flat?

V.   Yes, there was. I gave her the pension book and I asked
     her to pay things off for me. Instead of that she went
     and drew the pension and when I asked her, she
     turned to me and said she'd had the bailiffs come to
     the house and she'd had to pay them with it and
     therefore my bills were left.

I.   So how much money had she actually cashed?

V.   She had cashed £184.

I.   And you never got this back?

V.   No.

I.   Did you ever ask her what had happened to the money.

V.   When I mention it there's nothing said. They never
     mention nothing, none of them. She promised she
     was going to pay me off at £5 per week. I've never
     seen a fiver and while I have been in this home she
     has rung up and asked me for money in here.

I.   Did you know at the time that she had gone to pay the
     bailiffs or did you think that she had paid your gas
     and electric bills?

V.   She just said she'd took the money to pay the bailiffs so I
     don't know what had got done.

I.   How did you find out that your bills hadn't been paid by
     her?

V.   Well I found out and then I had to get in touch with my
     social worker. The gas and electric people got in

touch with her and then she found out for me. They've had £300 off me while I've been in here to pay off the bills.

I.   That's a lot of money isn't it? How much do you actually get a week?

V.   £9.40 a week.

I.   How did you actually feel when you found out Cath hadn't paid your bills and you had all these debts?

V.   I just did nothing else but cry, cry, cry and couldn't face anybody.

I.   Had she got a lot of debts herself do you think?

V.   Well she says she hasn't now so I don't know.

I.   Did she used to have?

V.   Yes.

I.   What sort of debts did she have, any idea?

V.   No I haven't. Once she did have the gas and the electric because they were both cut off.

I.   Was that at the time that she took the money from you?

V.   Yes, she said that she was in trouble but that was beside the point. She had had my money and therefore my bills should have been paid.

I.   Did you ever ask her directly to get the money back

V.   I have asked her time and time and time and I just get no answer now.

I.   Does she change the subject when you ask her?

V.   Yes. She says she's got no money and one thing and another but yet they can keep having new things. That's what gets me mad.

I.   What sort of new things do they buy?

V.   Well new clothes and one thing and another.

I.   Do they buy things for their house?

V.   Yes. When Gail went up the other Saturday she said they were doing the bathroom and that. I tell you she's all right if you're giving. You see I've rung up to school to Lee twice last week and told him to tell your mam to ring me or ask your mam to come to see me. I've had no reply and she sent Thomas up the week before

that to ask me if I'd got anything and I said no so of
course she doesn't know me now.

I. When you say anything, you mean money?

V. Yes.

I. Did Thomas come up on his own?

V. Yes.

I. And how old is Thomas now?

V. 10 or 11. But you see he catches the bus straight outside
their door and he goes straight back you see.

I. Have you any advice for other people like yourself who
lose money to relatives?

V. I don't know. The only thing I can say is not to do it
without getting written authority because you can
never get it back if you haven't got written authority.

I. Do you regret giving Cath the money?

V. I do, yes, I do. When you come to look at it, when I sit
here sometimes and think of what I've lent. I've lent
about £600 or more. It's a lot of money. I'd lost my
husband and he left me that bit of money to see me
through and I helped them out.

I. And have you any savings left?

V. No, nothing at all. Nothing.

I. So what do you do when you actually want a new dress
or anything like that?

V. I save what I can here or Gail's very good. She goes
round the shops and she'll say well I've bought you
this one and she'll say you pay me back at so much a
week so I do that but I try and save out of the money
that I get here.

I. Which is £9.40 a week?

V. Yes.

I. Do the rest of the family know what Cath's done to you?

V. Well Gail knows but Paul doesn't know.

I. Paul's your son?

V. Yes.

I. And what does Gail say about it?

V.   Gail's very cross. She says that I've never got to do it any more. She says she's fed up of telling me about doing it and therefore I don't do it no more because I'll never get it back. Gail says all Cath wants you for is for what she can get off you.

I.   At the time that Cath was taking money off you did you tell anybody about it?

V.   No, I kept it to myself and then one day I just happened to say to Gail I'd no money and Gail said where's your money go? Where's your pension or something so I just told her well Cath's borrowed it. Gail said that Cath's had bailiffs. It was when I was smoking and I was waiting and I thought she'd be here in a bit because she'll bring me a packet of cigarettes out of my pension. When she came, I said have you brought me some smokes? She said no. I said, what? She said no. I said I was wanting a cigarette, where's my pension? She said I haven't got any for you. I said what do you mean you haven't got any for me? She said well I've had to go and draw it and I've had to borrow it because bailiffs had been and I had to have it for such and such a time so I've gone and used your pension so you'll have to wait until I can get you some. Years before that I sent money to Cath's husband when he was in the army. He said when I come out of the army I'll have a gratuity, you know, a gratuity money and I'll give it you back as soon as I come out. When they came out of the army nothing was mentioned. When I asked for it one day, what did they do? A right big row because they had come to stop at my house, you see, and a right big row come.

I.   Who was the row between?

V.   Between me and him because I'd asked for the money. And what did I get? Black eyes and one thing and another.

I.   He hit you?

V.   Yes he did. And I've got witnesses to that. The lady who lived above in the flat. She told me to fetch the police in because they made my face into such a state. She said are you all right? Whatever has he done? She

said go and get the police. I said no. Go and get the
police love, she said. Don't let him get away with it
but I did.

I. And what injuries did you actually have?

V. I had a black eye and he went and banged all my lip up.
You see you know with me having the heart attack
that's what she was frightened of so she got in between him and then she was getting bruised you see,
on her really.

I. Was Cath there when he hit you?

V. Yes.

I. And what did she do?

V. She stood in between him to keep away from me because
of my heart and that. And he bumped her in the chest.

I. Do you wish you had got the police involved?

V. Yes, I do. I do wish I had got them in.

I. Was that the only time he hit you?

V. Yes. But I knew he'd hit me. He'd been out for the afternoon and he came back with this red car and he came
in and he was with one of his mates. He'd had plenty
to drink. Cath asked him whose the car was and he
said his. She asked him where he'd gotten it from and
I don't know what he said. He reckoned to have gone
to get some money. He said so I'll have some money
then. Of course I hadn't got any so off he went and
then it got from one thing to another and next thing
he started and that was it. He had hit me and later on
at night a fellow came through the door and asked if
he was in. I said he's not here. So I fetched the fellow
in and let him see what had happened. When it came
to, it was this fellow that he'd gotten the car off and
he had come to get some money off him for the car
you see.

I. What happened about the car?

V. Well what I heard was that he found out that I said I
thought he'd gone to his dad's, you see, so this fellow
must have gone up to find him and got him and he
took the car off him this same night.

I. You've said that you've kept a lot to yourself. Do you think it would have been better if you had actually told somebody at the time.

V. I do, yes, I do love. I do. I think perhaps I might not have been as poorly and not as I have been. I know if her dad had been alive she wouldn't dared done half of what she's done to me but her dad used to say to me at times, when she was younger and I used to say oh give up picking on her Bert. You're always picking on her. You'll regret the day, my lady, when she's older. You'll wish I had told her because she's going to mess you about right if you don't let me correct her. Sometimes I wish I had done. I do.

I. If there are people like yourself that are being abused physically and financially who would you tell them to confide in?

V. I would tell them to confide in the social worker if they possibly could.

I. What if they haven't got a social worker?

V. I should tell them to try and get in touch with the police or somebody like that or try and see if they've got any children who could talk to them.

Part II

The Exercises

6 What is Abuse?
The Exercises

Exercise 6.1 **Abuse**

Exercise 6.2 **Elder Abuse**

Exercise 6.3 **Professional Dilemmas**

Exercise 6.4 **Guidelines (1)**

Exercise 6.5 **Guidelines (2)**

Exercise 6.6 **The Multidisciplinary Approach**

Exercise 6.7 **The Police Perspective**

Exercise 6.1 Abuse

Learning objectives

To consider abuse in general terms. To look at learner's own values and perceptions.

Learner activities

1. Think about the term 'abuse'.
2. Make a list of what abuse (in general) means to you.
3. Write about an incident in your own life in which you consider you were abused. Explain why you felt you were abused.

Trainer activities

1. Make a list of what abuse means to you.
2. Relate an incident where you consider you were abused.

Assessment

1. Discuss lists and incidents.
2. Try to decide why incidents were considered to be abusive and by whom.
3. Consider whether other people would have perceived the incidents differently.

Exercise 6.2. Elder Abuse

Learning objectives

To clarify what constitutes elder abuse.

Learner activities

1. Think about the term 'elder abuse'.
2. Make a list of what elder abuse means to you.

Trainer activities

1. Make a list of what elder abuse means to you.

Assessment

1. Discuss lists.
2. After discussion present learner with Eastman's definition and the definition from the Social Services Inspectorate.

Suggested reading

1. Chapter 2 'What is old age abuse?' in Eastman, M. (1984) *Old Age Abuse,* London: Age Concern.
2. Social Services Inspectorate (1993) *No Longer Afraid: The Safeguard of Older People in Domestic Settings.* London: HMSO.

Exercise 6.3 Professional Dilemmas

Learning objectives

The aim of this exercise is first to ensure that the learner understands the concept of a professional dilemma, then to consider actual dilemmas in order to improve practice.

This exercise can be carried out either by an individual, in pairs, or in groups during a workshop. For additional material see Chapter 9.

Suggested reading

1. Riley, Patricia 'Professional dilemmas'. (Unpublished work 1989).

Learner activities

1. Read the definition of a professional dilemma.
2. Consider the situation described on the card which you have been given.
3. Write a statement about what you would do or not do.
4. State your reasons for doing or not doing.
5. Feedback either to trainer, other pairs or group.

Trainer activities

1. Give learner/pairs/group a card which describes a professional dilemma.

Assessment

1. Discuss outcomes.
2. Trainer to assess whether learner(s) actions were appropriate.

Exercise 6.4 Guidelines (1)

Learning objectives

To consider how some Social Services Departments define elder abuse.

Student activities

1. In your own words write in one sentence a general definition of elder abuse.
2. On one side of A4 paper, write a more detailed definition of elder abuse which could be used as a summary in a Social Services Department's guidelines.

Trainer activities

Discuss the value of having definitions/guidelines within a Social Services Department.

Assessment

Discuss the learner's written material.

Exercise 6.5 Guidelines (2)

Learning objectives

As in exercise 6.4.

Suggested reading

1. B.A.S.W. (1990) *Abuse of elderly people—guidelines for action.* Birmingham: B.A.S.W.
2. Kent Social Services Department (1987) *Practice guidelines for dealing with elder abuse* (see Appendix 1)
3. London Borough of Enfield (1993) *Notes of guidance (practice and procedure). Abuse of vulnerable adults* (see Appendix 2).
4. Social Services Inspectorate (1993) *No Longer Afraid: The Safeguard of Older People in Domestic Settings.* London: HMSO.

Learner activities

1. Write a critical analysis of the definitions used in the above mentioned guidelines.

Trainer activities

1. Present your own views on the definitions used in the guidelines mentioned above.

Assessment

1. Discuss learner's critical analysis.
2. Rewrite definitions for social services department's guidelines.

Exercise 6.6 The Multidisciplinary Approach

Learning objectives

Having already considered what constitutes elder abuse from one's own viewpoint, it is now necessary to learn how other professionals/agencies perceive elder abuse. The purpose of this exercise is to find out how other professionals define elder abuse and then to gain an initial insight into their ways of working with actual cases of elder abuse.

Suggested reading

1. Chapter 7 'Professional Perceptions' in Eastman, M.(1984) *Old Age Abuse*, London: Age Concern.

Learner activities

1. Make a list of questions which could be used when interviewing another professional person about the concept of elder abuse.
2. Conduct interviews with various professionals.
3. Write a brief summary of each interview.
4. Attend as an observer a multidisciplinary case conference/case discussion.
5. Spend time observing professionals with abused clients.

Trainer activities

1. Set up interviews for learner with other professionals e.g. consultant, general practitioner, social worker, district nurse, community psychiatric nurse, health visitor, local authority residential worker, day centre worker and police.
2. Observe learner during an interview.
3. Arrange observation visits with professionals.

Assessment

1. Discuss interviews and observation visits.
2. Feedback on interviewing skills.

Exercise 6.7 The Police Perspective

Learning objectives

To understand which practices constitute abuse from a police perspective.

Suggested reading

1. Age Concern (1986) *The Law and Vulnerable Elderly People*. London: Age Concern.
2. Section 2.5 in London Borough of Enfield (1993) *Notes of guidance (practice and procedure). Abuse of vulnerable adults* (see Appendix 2).

Learner activities

1. Read written material and discuss with trainer.
2. Meet with police either from the Community Liaison Department or abuse unit who have experience of working with abuse cases, i.e. children, rape victims etc.
3. Write a summary of key points raised in the meeting with police.

Trainer activities

1. Provide written material and discuss.
2. Set up meeting for learner with appropriate police personnel.

Assessment

Discuss meeting and summary.

7 Recognizing Abuse
The Exercises

Exercise 7.1 **Injuries**

Exercise 7.2 **Who is at risk?**

Exercise 7.3 **Reactions to abuse**

Exercise 7.4 **Social and economic factors**

Exercise 7.5 **Developing skills**

Exercise 7.6 **Financial abuse**

Exercise 7.7 **Institutional abuse**

Exercise 7.8 **Signs of institutional abuse**

Exercise 7.9 **Stress and carers**

Exercise 7.1 Injuries

Learning objectives

To make the learner think about the kind of injuries which could be caused in a physically abusive situation.

Suggested reading

1. Refer back to local authority guidelines.
2. Hocking, E.D. (1988), 'Miscare—a form of abuse in the elderly', *Update*, 15th May 2411–2419.
3. Decalmer, P. (1993) 'Clinical presentation'. In P. Decalmer and F. Glendenning (eds) *The mistreatment of elderly people.* London: Sage.
4. Davies, M. (1993) 'Recognising abuse: an assessment tool for nurses'. In P. Decalmer and F. Glendenning (eds) *The mistreatment of elderly people.* London: Sage

Learner activities

1. Make a list of injuries which could be inflicted non-accidentally.
2. Indicate on a body chart (see Appendix 3) where you would expect to find non-accidental injuries.

Trainer activities

1. Provide slides, photographs of injuries, body chart and discuss.
2. If possible arrange for the learner to see actual injuries on a ward or in a Casualty Department.
3. Demonstrate how injuries can be inflicted and on which parts of the body.

Assessment

Discuss list, body chart and any injuries seen.

Exercise 7.2 Who Is At Risk?

Learning objectives

For the learner to consider who may be a victim or abuser in our society.

Suggested reading

1. Pillemer, K. and Finkelhor, D. (1988), 'The prevalence of elder abuse: a random sample survey'. *The Gerontologist* Vol. 28 No. 1, 51–57.

2. Pritchard, J.H. (1989) 'Confronting the taboo of the abuse of elderly people' *Social Work Today*, 5th October 12–13.

3. Pritchard, J.H. (1990) 'Old and Abused' *Social Work Today,* 15th February 22–23.

4. Pritchard, J.H. (1993) 'Gang warfare', *Community Care*, 8th July, 22–23.

5. Pritchard, J.H. (1993) 'Dispelling some myths', *Journal of Elder Abuse and Neglect, 5*, No.2, 27–36.

6. Sengstock M.C. and Barrett, (Spring 1986) 'Elderly victims of family abuse, neglect and maltreatment: Can legal assistance help?' *Journal of Gerontological Social Work* Vol. 9 (3) 43–61.

Learner activities

1. Write a stereotype description of a person who you think is a 'typical victim'.

2. Write a stereotype description of a person who you think is a 'typical abuser'.

Trainer activities

1. Discuss learner's stereotype descriptions.

2. Introduce concept of

   a. carers abusing dependant older people and

   b. deliberate pre-meditated abuse.

Assessment

Use and discuss scenarios to illustrate people at risk and their abusers (see Chapter 14).

Exercise 7.3 Reactions to Abuse

Learning objectives

For the learner to consider how a victim may react to being abused.

To develop knowledge in looking for signs of abuse.

Suggested reading

1. Eastman, M. (October 1988), 'Granny abuse'. *Community Outlook*, 15–16.

Learner activities

1. Read two case files where clients have been physically abused.
2. Make a list of how you would expect an older person to react, having been abused.

Trainer activities

Provide two case files for learner to study.

Assessment

Discuss cases and learner's list.

Exercise 7.4 Social and Economic Factors

Learning objectives

There is no single causal factor of abuse. The aim of this exercise is to broaden the learner's perception about circumstances in which abuse may occur.

Suggested reading

1. Bookin D. and Dunkle R.E. (January 1985) 'Elder abuse: issues for the practitioner'. *Social Casework: the Journal of Contemporary Social Work,* 3–12.
2. Hickey T. and Douglass R.L. (1981), 'Neglect and abuse of older family members: professionals' perspectives and case experiences'. *The Gerontologist* Vol. 21, No. 2, 171–176.

Learner activities

1. Read suggested reading material.
2. Read two cases provided by trainer.
3. Write a social history on each case.
4. Briefly summarize why the histories were different.

Trainer activities

1. Provide suggested reading material.
2. Provide two cases which came from different social/economic backgrounds.

Assessment

1. Discuss cases.
2. Make joint list of social and economic factors which may be causal factors in abuse.

Exercise 7.5 Developing Skills

Learning objectives

This exercise is designed to assess whether the learner has started to develop skills in recognizing signs of abuse.

Learner activities

1. Read scenario provided by trainer.
2. Make a list of signs and symptoms which would indicate abuse is taking place.

Trainer activities

1. Provide scenario which illustrates signs and symptoms of physical abuse.

Assessment

1. Discuss learner's assessment of the situation.
2. Discuss what actually happened.

Exercise 7.6 Financial Abuse

Learning objectives

To teach the learner the complexities of working with cases of financial abuse.

Learner activities

1. Read summaries of cases of financial abuse.
2. Meet with home care organizer to discuss cases and procedures.
3. Write a checklist of difficulties in working with cases of financial abuse and who can help.

Trainer activities

1. Provide and discuss summaries of financial abuse cases.
2. Organize meeting with home care organizer who has dealt with cases of financial abuse.

Assessment

1. Discuss meeting and checklist provided by learner.

Exercise 7.7 Institutional Abuse

Learning objectives

To consider what constitutes institutional abuse.

Suggested reading

1. Bedford Social Services Department—'Local project; the residential perspective' in *The Abuse of Elderly People* (1989), 24–31, 47–50.

Learner activities

1. Make a list of institutions where abuse could take place.
2. Make a list of activities which you would consider to be abusive in an institution.

Assessment

1. Discuss lists in training sessions.

Exercise 7.8 Signs of Institutional Abuse

Learning objectives

To develop skills in recognizing institutional abuse.

Suggested reading

1. London Borough of Enfield (1993). *Notes of guidance (practice and procedure). Abuse of vulnerable adults,* section 5 (see Appendix 2).

Learner activities

1. Discuss with trainer lists from suggested reading.
2. Meet with local authority and health authority officials who have investigated abuse in residential institutions.
3. Make list of points raised in meetings.

Trainer activities

1. Set up meetings with people who have been responsible for investigating abuse in institutions.

Assessment

1. Discuss learner's list of points.

Exercise 7.9 Stress and Carers

Learning objectives

To consider what stresses may push a carer to abuse an older person.

Suggested reading

1. Crossroads Care (May 1990) *Caring for carers: a nationwide survey.* London: Monica Hart Press and public relations.
2. Garrett, G. (August 1986), 'Old age abuse by carers'. *The Professional Nurse*, 304–305.
3. Homer, A.C. and Gilleard, C. (1990), 'Abuse of elderly people by their carers'. *British Medical Journal* 301, 1359–1362.
4. Pritchard, J.H. (1990), 'Charting the Hits', *Care Weekly*, 19th Oct, 10–11.
5. Sanford, J.R.A. (1975), 'Tolerance of debility in elderly dependants by supporters at home: its significance for hospital practice'. *British Medical Journal*, 23rd August, 471–473.

Learner activities

1. Read case studies where (a) a carer has abused an older person and (b) the carer has been abused.
2. Meet with carer(s). Write a summary of findings.
3. If possible observe a relatives' support group. Write a summary of observations.
4. Meet with a representative from the local Alzheimer's Disease Society. Write a summary of findings.

Trainer activities

1. Provide case studies.
2. Set up meetings for learner with carer(s), relatives support group, representative from Alzheimer's Disease Society.
3. Observe learner in one interview.
4. Discuss in training sessions (a) dementia, (b) stress.

Assessment

1. Discuss learner's summaries of findings and observations.
2. Feedback on interviewing skills.

8 Working With Abuse
The Exercises

Exercise 8.1 **Resources**

Exercise 8.2 **The Law**

Exercise 8.3 **Monday morning in-tray**

Exercise 8.4 **Interviewing skills**

Exercise 8.5 **At risk register**

Exercise 8.6 **The case conference**

Exercise 8.1 Resources

Learning objectives

To find out what resources are provided locally for abused older people.

Learner activities

1 . Make a list of resources which you think might be used in a case of elder abuse. Discuss with trainer.

2. Make visits to places which provide a resource for older people who have been abused, e.g. day centre, day hospital, old people's home, hospital ward (providing respite care), night shelter, fostering/family placement scheme.

3. Discuss elder abuse and procedures with staff.

4. Find out if there are any specialist counsellors and therapists in the local area, who could work with victims and/or abusers. Make a list.

5. Write summary of visits and what resources are provided.

6. Make a list of gaps in resources for abused older people.

Trainer activities

1. Arrange visits for learner to resource centres.

Assessment

1. Discuss visits, summaries and gaps in services.

Exercise 8.2 The Law

Learning objectives

Professionals actually have very little power to protect older people from being abused. It is necessary for the learner to understand what procedures can be followed.

Suggested reading

1. Re-read local authority guidelines.
2. Age Concern (1986) *The Law and Vulnerable Elderly People.* London: Age Concern
3. Griffiths, A., Roberts, G. and Williams, J. (1993) 'Elder abuse and the law'. In P. Decalmer and F. Glendenning (eds) *The Mistreatment of Elderly People.* London: Sage.
4. Gostin, L. (1983). *A Practical Guide to Mental Health Law.* London: MIND.
5. Law Commission (1991) *Mentally Incapacitated Adults and Decision Making: An Overview.* London: HMSO.
6. Law Commission (l993) *Mentally Incapacitated and Other Vulnerable Adults. Public Law Protection. Consultation paper No 130.* London: HMSO.
7. London Borough of Enfield (l993) *Notes of guidance (practice and procedure). Abuse of vulnerable adults.* Section 2.5. (See Appendix 2)
8. Public Trust Office (1989) *Procedure notes and forms on the work of the Court of Protection and Protection Division.* London: Public Trust Office.
9. Sengstock, M.C. and Barrett, S. (Spring 1986), 'Elderly victims of family abuse, neglect and maltreatment: can legal assistance help?' *Journal of Gerontological Social Work* Vol.9 (3), 43–61.

Learner activities

1. Read written material.
2. Interview
    (a) local authority court officer
    (b) solicitor

   (c) police (from various settings e.g. abuse unit, CID, community based, victim support officer)

  3. Write summary of interviews.

Trainer activities

  1. Provide written material.

  2. Arrange interviews with court officer, solicitor.

Assessment

  1. Discuss interviews and summaries provided by learner.

Exercise 8.3 Monday Morning In-tray

This exercise is specifically designed for social services staff.

Learning objectives

To learn how to prioritize and to consider relevant factors when prioritizing.

This exercise can be carried out either in an individual supervision/training session, in pairs or in groups during a workshop. For additional material see Chapter 10.

Learner activities

1. You are employed by a social services department and specialize in working with older people.
2. You are given five cards which are the referrals/messages you find in your tray when you arrive at work on Monday morning.
3. Write down in detail how you would proceed and your reasons for doing so.
4. Feedback to trainer and/or other groups.

Trainer activities

1. Give learner/group five cards.

Assessment

1. Discuss actions/procedures.

Exercise 8.4 Interviewing Skills

Learning objectives

To develop skills in interviewing victims or abusers in cases of elder abuse. This is to be achieved through role play. *For additional material see Chapter 11.*

Learner activities

1. Consider the role you are given for five minutes.
2. Engage in role play for 10 minutes.
3. Discuss the role play.

Learner activities

1. Provide role play cards.
2. Observe role play.

Assessment

1. Discuss learner's role play participation.

Exercise 8.5 At Risk Register

Learning objectives

To consider the value of having an at risk register for older people. To develop the criteria for such a register.

Suggested reading

1. Departmental child protection manual.
2. Solihull Joint Consultative Committee (1993) *Guidelines for Managing Abuse of Vulnerable Adults.*

Learner activities

1. Read suggested material.
2. Make a list of advantages and disadvantages of having an at risk register for older people.
3. Develop a list of criteria for an at risk register.

Trainer activities

1. Discuss child protection procedures with learner before s/he undertakes activities 2 and 3.

Assessment

1. Discuss written work produced by learner.

Exercise 8.6 The Case Conference

Learning objectives

To convene a case conference which involves the subject being an older person who has been abused.

To develop skills in participating in a case conference.

This is a group exercise. For additional material see Chapter 12.

Learner activities

1. Read information sheet on case.
2. Read about the role you are to play.
3. Participate in case conference for 30 minutes.
4. Feedback about role play and the decision(s) from the case conference.

Trainer activities

1. Provide material for the case conference.
2. Observe the participants in the case conference.

Assessment

1. Trainer to feedback on observations from the case conference.
2. Discuss learners' participation.

9 Professional Dilemmas

The concept of the 'professional dilemma' was introduced in Chapter 1. This chapter contains material which could be used by trainers in conjunction with Exercise 6.3.

Notes for trainers

- This exercise can be carried out by an individual, in pairs or in groups.
- The following pages contain information about situations which could cause a professional dilemma. Each dilemma needs to be written on an individual card.
- Each participant needs to be given an instruction card which states the following:

    1. A professional dilemma is a situation in which a person who has a specialist knowledge is confronted by choices between equally unacceptable alternatives. It is about **doing** and sometimes about **not doing.**
    2. Read the situation described on the card which has been given to you.
    3. Consider what you would do or not do.
    4. Write down your reasons for doing or not doing.
    5. You have 15 minutes for this exercise.
    6. Feedback to trainer/other groups.

- Each participant needs to be given a card describing a professional dilemma.
- The exercise will run for 15 minutes.
- Participants will then feedback to trainer/groups.

Professional dilemmas

You have been visiting Mrs Hitchins every week for three months and during the past month you have noticed one black eye, a bruise on her neck and a cut lip. Mrs Hitchins says she keeps going dizzy and falling over. According to her general practitioner she is fit and healthy apart from a bit of arthritis in her knees. Mrs Hitchins lives with her husband.

You are a new housing officer, who has been told that you must visit Grace Hancock to discuss her rent arrears which now total £1000. Mrs Hancock has a history of arrears. Her grandson takes responsibility for paying the rent and has previously reduced the arrears when approached by your department. Today you have to talk to Mrs Hancock about the possibility of eviction. When you do this she tells you that her grandson has huge financial problems and she does not want to get him into trouble.

Arthur suffers from schizophrenic episodes. He is the primary carer for his disabled wife, Ethel, who is bedridden. During his periods of illness he does not care for his wife at all. Ethel is not fed and is left to lie in urine and faeces. The neglect becomes serious and life threatening but is not willful on Arthur's part.

You are a warden who goes in to get Mrs Adams dressed every morning and you put her to bed at night. Mrs Adams lives with her 38-year-old son. One Sunday morning Mrs Adams tells you her son has raped her. You laugh it off because Mrs Adams has started to dement. The following two Sundays but never on a week day she tells you the same thing.

Seventy-year-old Miss Hutchinson has cared for her younger sister, Alice, for the past five years. Alice suffers from severe senile dementia. She is doubly incontinent and repeatedly asks 'when are we going to school again?' You have often suspected that Miss Hutchinson reaches the end of her tether and hits her sister but she always says that she is coping. One day you arrive and Miss Hutchinson admits that she has just burnt Alice with a hot brush because she would not sit still while having her hair done.

You are a care assistant in a local authority old people's home. You know there is another care assistant, Sue, who is deliberately cruel to Eric, one of the residents. You have seen Sue pinch Eric viciously several times. She often ignores him when he asks to go to the toilet and then shouts at him when he wets himself.

You are a student nurse working on an acute elderly ward. During your first week you begin to think that Staff Nurse Young is 'a bit rough' with Nellie Holmes. During the second week you walk into the toilet and you see Staff Nurse slap Nellie across the face.

You are on your final placement as a student social worker and your last placement report was not very good. Early on in the placement you were given an assessment to do and successfully set up a day centre for Mr Realms. You are on the point of closing the case when you get a telephone call from the day centre worker saying Mr Realms has 'funny marks on his hand' which he thinks could be cigarette burns. Your practice teacher tells you not to bother about the phone call and just to get on with closing the case.

You are a home care organizer and one of your home helps has regularly been using her own money to buy food for a lady whose son refuses to leave money in the house. He says he buys food for his mother but there is never any evidence of this in the house. You have already told the home help to stop using her own money.

You have been working as a housing officer in this area for many years. Sometimes you pop in to see Mr McCreadie when you are passing by. As you knock on the open door you hear shouting. After knocking several times, you are quite concerned at the intensity of the shouting. You walk through the door, announcing yourself. As you walk in the lounge you see

Mr McCreadie being hit with a slipper across his face by his son.

Mr and Mrs Evans have been married for 40 years. Mr Evans physically abuses his wife and always has done so. Mrs Evans talks openly to you about his attacks but says he cannot help it because 'it's in his blood'. She refuses to do anything about the abuse.

You have known Lydia for quite some time and when you see her on her own she is always very chatty and welcomes your support. However, on the few occasions you have seen Lydia with her daughter, who lives around the corner and is the primary carer, Lydia is a different person. She is totally withdrawn and flinches if her daughter comes near her. When you have talked to Lydia about this she denies that she is frightened of her daughter.

George was physically beaten by his daughter-in-law who demanded that he pay her £30 per week for doing his shopping and cleaning the house. When he refused he ended up in hospital with broken ribs. He made a statement to the police but when discharged from hospital withdrew his statement and refused to talk about the incident. You first met George when you were the duty social worker during the initial investigation. You have now been allocated the case.

You are visiting Edna Shawcross today to discuss her request to be rehoused in a sheltered accommodation complex. You are shown into the lounge by Edna's daughter, Sylvia. While you are waiting to see Edna, you hear Sylvia say to her mother in the next room 'Come on you stupid cow, can't you hurry up? You are bloody useless'.

You attend a social work team allocation meeting. Your team leader wants you to take a case which requires a nursery application for a three-year-old boy. There is another case which has been referred by a general practitioner who suspects an 89-year-old woman is being physically abused by a member of her family. Your team leader does not like working with older people and says the case is not a priority and can wait another week.

You are a health visitor. You are visiting a family where a 24-year-old mother is looking after a family of children aged four, two years and three months, plus a grandmother aged 86 who is starting to dement. The last time you visited you noticed that the grandmother was badly bruised on the face. When you ask about it the young mother said her gran had fallen out of the wheel chair. Gran said it was a lie and that she had been hit by her granddaughter.

Mrs Alessi has come into the Housing Area office to ask if she can be rehoused quickly. She has a black eye and is badly bruised on the left side of her face. When you ask her why she wants to move, she says has her reasons, but she cannot tell you.

Mr Sampson has suffered several strokes and is severely disabled. He has respite care in hospital every five weeks. He lives with his wife who is extremely houseproud in a luxurious bungalow. However Mr Sampson is forced to exist in the smallest bedroom where there is only a bed and commode. He is not allowed anywhere else in the bungalow. You are the new district nurse who has to visit twice a week in order to open Mr Sampson's bowels. Mrs Sampson asks you not to do this because 'it makes a terrible mess'. It seems the previous district nurse has colluded with Mrs Sampson over the years.

You are a hospital social worker. Mrs Tunney has had frequent admissions to hospital over the past year and from the information you have received from the domiciliary services and reports from neighbours you suspect that Mrs Tunney is being beaten by her son but is too terrified to say anything. Mrs Tunney would like to go into an old people's home. You think there may be a vacancy in three week's time. The consultant wants to discharge this lady in a couple of days. He does not believe that elder abuse exists and also thinks highly of Mrs Tunney's son who is a very successful businessman.

10 Monday Morning In-tray

This exercise has been designed specifically for social services staff who are constantly under pressure and find there are never enough hours in the working day. The aim of the exercise is to help the learner develop ways of prioritizing work.

Notes for trainers

- This exercise can be carried out by an individual, in pairs or in groups.
- On the following pages information is given about referrals and messages. Each referral/message needs to be written on an individual card.
- Each participant needs to be given an instruction card which states the following:
    1. You are employed by a social services department and specialize in working with the elderly.
    2. You have five cards which are the referrals/messages you find in your tray when you arrive at work on Monday morning.
    3. Write down in detail how you would proceed and your reasons for doing so.
    4. You have 30 minutes for this exercise.
    5. Feedback to trainer/other groups.

- Each participant needs to be given five referrals/messages.
- The exercise will run for 30 minutes.
- Participants will then feedback to trainers/groups.

Referrals/messages

Monday is your duty day. At 10.00 a.m. you are asked to go to interview a 75-year-old woman who has presented in casualty. She has been in casualty four times in the past three weeks. Today she has broken her leg, having fallen down the stairs.

Dr. Bennett, consultant geriatrician, telephones you. He wants you to go out on a domiciliary visit as soon as possible. He is concerned that one of his ex-respite patients is being neglected by her schizophrenic husband.

You should have done a home visit to Mrs Hayes last week after she had had a temporary stay in Valley Meadows old people's home. She is a very anxious lady who cannot decide if she wants Part III accommodation or not.

Sister Byrne rings you up about Mrs Bates, a 63-year-old woman who is regularly battered by her husband. Mrs Bates is about to discharge herself and ward staff want to prevent this. You have a good relationship with Mrs Bates and may be able to persuade her to stay a little longer.

You have been trying to meet with Mr Dyson's son for a long time. You are suspicious that the son is both neglecting and financially abusing his father. The home help telephones you to say she knows the son is going to visit the house in the next hour.

Mr Nelson has been physically abused by his daughter-in-law. He had broken ribs and cigarette burns. He willingly came into an old people's home for safety and made a statement to the police about what happened. You receive a phone call from the principal of the old people's home saying the son and daughter-in-law arrived and have persuaded Mr Nelson to go home with them.

Sister Blake rings after a ward round which you could not attend. Dr. Griffiths has decided to discharge Miss Emerson tomorrow. You think Miss Emerson is physically abused by her brother and have consistently voiced your concerns to Dr. Griffiths. You have been waiting for a Part III bed for Miss Emerson.

You have a colleague on your team who started six weeks ago as a level 1 worker, having just completed the Diploma in social work course. She has received a phone call at 9 o'clock this morning from a home help saying she has found Mr Evans covered in bruises. Your colleague needs to go out immediately but is petrified due to her lack of experience. She asks you if you can go with her.

Seventy-year-old Mr Richards cares for his wife, Ethel, who suffers from Alzheimer's disease. Most of the time he copes very well but there are occasions when he reaches the end of his tether and you think he could physically abuse Ethel. Mr Richards always telephones you and asks you to visit when he feels like this and so far you have been able to help just by listening to him. You receive a phone call from Mr Richards asking you to visit immediately because he feels like strangling Ethel.

Your team leader forgot to give you a message last week. The relatives of one of your clients, Lydia, had arranged to come into the office to see you. The relatives have Power of Attorney and are threatening to sell Lydia's flat and put her into a private nursing home. Lydia wants to remain in her flat.

You receive a phone call to say Miss Everton has been badly beaten and admitted to hospital. Her condition is unstable. She is asking to see you.

Mr Andrews has cared for his demented mother for the past five years. He has found this extremely difficult and on occasions he has hit her. Last week he poured a bowl of soup over her when she refused to eat and she had to be admitted with burns to the local hospital. There is a phone message from the local hospital saying Mr Andrews has now attempted suicide.

A warden rings you to say that 80-year-old Mr Humphries has received a letter from the electricity board threatening disconnection in two days' time. It seems no-one has paid the electricity bills for some time and there are arrears totalling £300.

A day centre worker had rung late Friday afternoon after you had left the office. She was concerned about Lilian, who has been a client of yours for several years. Lilian had been crying all day in the centre but would not talk to anybody and refused to eat anything. She is normally a pleasant, sociable lady.

Mr Amis, who is dementing, has battered his wife all their married life. You have been monitoring the situation as Mrs Amis refuses any practical help. There is a telephone message from Mrs Amis asking you to visit as soon as possible.

11 Role Play Exercises

We all know that the most common reactions to the two words 'role play' are moans, groans, and withdrawal. However, we also know that people can learn a great deal from participating in role play once they have got over their initial self consciousness and embarrassment. The purpose of the following role play exercises is two-fold. First, to develop skills in communicating and interviewing either a victim or abuser. Second, for people to consider what it might feel like to be a victim or an abuser. The following pages describe particular roles which can be used in a role play exercise. Some of the roles can be adapted for any professional person e.g. social worker, district nurse, community psychiatric nurse, health visitor, physiotherapist, occupational therapist, consultant, general practitioner, nurse, warden, home help etc. Other roles are specifically for social services staff.

The Exercise

- Trainers need to prepare the information cards for participants before the exercise begins.
- Trainers should decide whether the role play takes place unobserved or observed by another person.
- Participants need to be given a card stating their role and some background information.
- Participants need five minutes to assimilate the information on their cards. They should not communicate with each other at this time.
- The role play should run for 10 minutes.

- After the role play has finished participants should discuss and analyze what has taken place.

Information For Trainers

- The following pages give information which can be used in different role play exercises.
- Ideally, each role should be typed/written on a card.
- An asterisk marks the roles which can be adapted for various professions. Trainers should insert the required role in the places marked by an asterisk.

ROLE PLAY 1

ROLE: Any professional ****

You have been visiting Mr and Mrs Higgins for the past six months. They are both in their eighties. You are suspicious that Mrs Higgins is physically abused by her husband. You know Mrs Higgins will be on her own this afternoon so you intend to confront her about this situation because on your last visit she had had a black eye and a cut on her chin.

ROLE: Mrs Higgins (aged 83)

You have been married to your husband for the past 63 years. He has always been violent towards you and has even hit your children on occasions. You are very ashamed about this and feel that you should have had the courage to leave him years ago. You are very surprised when the **** drops in unexpectedly. You know that he or she is going to ask you about the black eye and a cut on the chin you had last week. You have no intention of telling him/her that your husband does abuse you.

ROLE PLAY 2

ROLE: Any professional ****

You arrive to find Betty, aged 70, huddled in the corner of her lounge. She won't talk at all and is sobbing. How do you proceed?

ROLE: Betty (aged 70)

You have been sexually assaulted by your son, who is in his mid forties. He actually raped you last night and you are so confused about the situation that you have been sitting huddled in the corner of the lounge since the incident happened. A **** has come in and found you in the corner. You are sobbing but you refuse to talk.

ROLE PLAY 3

ROLE: Any professional ****

Celia is a slightly demented 78-year-old lady. You arrive for your weekly visit, expecting that you will have your normal cup of tea and general chat to see how Celia has been getting on.

ROLE: Celia (aged 78)

You are slightly demented and tend to go off at a tangent during conversation. You have a **** who visits once a week. As soon as s/he walks in today you say to him/her 'my brother raped me last night'.

ROLE PLAY 4

ROLE: Any professional ****

Sam looks extremely thin and always says he is hungry when you visit. On your last visit he said that his daughter starves him. The daughter says Sam 'eats like a horse'. You need to express your concerns to the daughter.

ROLE: Daughter of Sam

A **** has made an appointment to see you today to discuss the care of your father, Sam. You have seen this **** on several occasions and s/he is always asking about Sam's eating habits. One of your favourite expressions is Sam 'eats like a horse'.

ROLE PLAY 5

ROLE: Any professional ****

Today you have to talk to Peter, aged 25, who is schizophrenic. For the past five years Peter has been looking after his frail mother. During his schizophrenic episodes Peter neglects his mother and sometimes becomes very angry with her, so much so that he beats her. He has no memory of this. When he is feeling well he has a very loving relationship with his mother who is well cared for. You are very concerned about Peter and his mother but you need to explain to Peter what happens when he is ill.

ROLE: Peter (age 25)

You are a single man who suffers from schizophrenia. You live with your frail mother. When you are well you care for your mother very adequately but you cannot remember what you do when you are ill. You know that the **** is coming today to talk about what happens when you are ill.

ROLE PLAY 6

ROLE: Any professional ****

You are going to visit one of your clients in an old people's home. As you are walking along one of the corridors, you glance into a bedroom and you see a care assistant hit a resident. What do you say?

ROLE: Care assistant in an old people's home

You have just hit a resident across the face. Someone is walking along the corridor, has glanced in and seen you abuse the resident.

ROLE PLAY 7

ROLE: Any professional ****

You have been involved with Mr and Mrs Eaton for sometime now. Mrs Eaton is severely disabled and can only get about in a wheelchair. She is cared for by her husband who is in his sixties. Mrs Eaton has told you that her husband has a drink problem and that he becomes very violent when he is drunk. She wants you to talk to her husband about this. Today you are going to interview Mr Eaton on his own.

ROLE: Mr Eaton (aged mid sixties)

The **** has made an appointment to see you on your own today. Normally s/he visits both you and your wife. Mrs Eaton is severely disabled and wheelchair bound. You are the primary carer. You have a drink problem which you deny to both your wife and the **** . You have always drunk heavily but now you feel you need a drink more because of the stress you experience whilst caring for your wife.

ROLE PLAY 8

ROLE: Any professional ****

Over the past few weeks you have become increasingly worried about Mrs Black who is suffering from dementia and is cared for by her son. No matter what time of day you have visited recently, Mrs Black has been asleep. You suspect that her son, Mr Black, is giving her too much medication in order to sedate her. Today you need to confront Mr Black about this.

ROLE: Mr Black

You care for your mother who is suffering from dementia. You find your mother very difficult to cope with and you are becoming very depressed about the situation. The only way you can alleviate the stress is to drug your mother throughout the day and night. You have not told anybody that you are doing this. You do not think that you are doing your mother any harm because the doctor said the sleeping tablets are only mild.

ROLE PLAY 9

ROLE: Social worker

Sixty-two-year-old Doris has had enough of her husband who has battered her all her life. She has never told anyone about it before but has gradually confided in you. Today you need to explain the options/resources available to Doris in order to get her out of the situation.

ROLE: Doris (aged 62)

You have been battered all your life by your husband and you have now reached the end of your tether. You probably would have continued to stay in this situation had you not met the social worker who now visits you on a weekly basis. You have never told anyone before that your husband has battered you. Your children are unaware of the abuse and are extremely fond of their father. Over the past few months you have started to talk to the social worker about the physical violence. You feel that s/he may be able to help you get out of the situation.

ROLE PLAY 10

ROLE: Social worker

You have been involved with Alan and his father for a few months. You are pretty certain that Alan abuses his father physically. Today you are interviewing Alan in the social services area office. You have got to the point in the interview when Alan admits that he does hit his father when he 'plays up'.

ROLE: Alan (aged 50)

You are single and you live with your father in a council house where you have always lived. A social worker has been visiting for a few months and has arranged day care for your father. You don't trust this social worker as s/he keeps asking you if you are under stress. Today you are in the local social services area office and you have got to the point in the interview when you have admitted that you do hit your father when he 'plays up'. You now become very angry and storm about the office. You say to the social worker 'why shouldn't I hit him. He beat hell out of us kids when we were young'.

ROLE PLAY 11

ROLE: Social worker

You are visiting Mary who cares for her mother. You have already met the mother last week. She presented as a sweet, frail old lady. You are aware that Mary visits her mother three times a day as no services have been put in. You have come to assess how you can alleviate some of the pressure on Mary.

ROLE: Mary

You are very surprised when a social worker lands on your doorstep. You are not aware that s/he has visited your mother last week. You are at breaking point because your mother is confused. You have just made a cup of tea for yourself and the social worker. You open the conversation by saying 'I really hate my mother. I wish she would die'.

ROLE PLAY 12

ROLE: Social worker

You are on duty and you are asked to see in the office a 20-year-old man who says he needs advice about his great aunt who is disabled. You have already started the interview and taken some basic details. You now know that he lives with his aunt and has been the primary carer for the past six months.

ROLE: 20 year old man

You have come to see a duty social worker in the local area office. You have already said at the beginning of the interview that you care for your great aunt, who is disabled. You have been looking after your aunt for the past six months and you have come to tell the social worker that you cannot cope any longer and you are frightened of what you might do to her. You have already hit your aunt on several occasions but you are not going to tell the social worker this.

ROLE PLAY 13

ROLE: Social worker

Mr and Mrs Lally look after Vera, their neighbour who is confused. They have her pension book and supposedly pay all her bills. The gas and electricity supplies have been cut off during the past few days and the housing department have informed you that there are arrears amounting to £1,000. You need to discuss this with Mr and Mrs, Lally.

ROLE: Either Mr or Mrs Lally (aged early twenties)

You and your partner look after the old lady next door, Vera, who is very confused. You have her pension book and tell everybody that you pay all her bills. In fact you are financially abusing Vera. A social worker has called today and has asked if he or she can speak to you. Your partner is out and you are scared that the social worker is going to ask some awkward questions.

ROLE PLAY 14

ROLE: Social worker

You are waiting for Elizabeth to arrive at day centre because you have promised to visit her there. When she gets off the community transport mini-bus, she has a bleeding nose. The other people say the driver hit Elizabeth.

ROLE: Elizabeth (aged 75)

You are going to day centre. You are a bit slow on your feet due to arthritis and the mini-bus driver has lost his temper and hit you across the face. When you arrive at day centre, your nose is bleeding and your social worker is waiting for you as arranged. The other people on the mini-bus tell your social worker what has happened. You admit the driver did hit you but you do not want it taken any further.

ROLE: Mini-bus driver

You hate your job as mini-bus driver taking older people to day centres. This was the only job you could get and you are fed up with your wife's nagging, about all the debts the family have. You have no patience with older people and today you got fed up with Elizabeth who is very slow and you hit her across the face. When the social worker confronts you, you have a couldn't-care-less attitude.

ROLE PLAY 15

ROLE: Social worker/doctor/nurse ****

Frances has been severely battered by her daughter. She has a broken arm, lacerations on her face and her hearing has been affected by blows to the side of her head. Frances was found by the home help and admitted to hospital. You now have to interview her daughter. How do you begin?

ROLE: Daughter of Frances

A **** has come to interview you. You guess that it is about your mother whom you have physically beaten the day before. You know your mother has been admitted to hospital but you do not know the extent of the injuries as you have not visited her. You intend to be ignorant about the situation and are going to deny that you saw your mother yesterday.

12 The Case Conference

The purpose of convening a case conference is to provide a multi-disciplinary forum where information can be exchanged. Professionals often find themselves attending a case conference without having had any training about why case conferences can be useful, on procedures in convening a conference or on how to present information in a coherent way. The purpose of this exercise is to give learners the opportunity to practice and learn through role play.

Notes for trainers

- This is a group exercise.
- Information about the case needs to be given to each participant. Participants should not discuss the information between themselves at this stage.
- Each participant should be given a role and information regarding this role. Again, participants should not discuss this information.
- Each participant will be given a label to wear during the case conference, indicating who they are.
- Participants should have 5 to 10 minutes to assimilate the information.

- Participants will go into the case conference setting and a chairperson will be selected.

- The case conference will be convened for 30 minutes.

- The chairperson will be asked to feedback on the discussion and decisions at the end of the conference.

- Participants will discuss performance and outcome.

This exercise can be particularly useful when two or three conferences are convened at the same time using the same case material. Feedback is then conducted group by group and a full discussion follows.

Prior to the exercise commencing trainers and participants should decide whether the victim/carer should be invited to attend the case conference.

CASE CONFERENCE 1

INFORMATION (to be given to all participants)

SUBJECT: *Edith Middleton*

AGE: *80*

Edith has been admitted to hospital as an emergency. She has fallen down the stairs and has suffered a damaged spine. She says she lost her balance. Edith is mentally sound, not confused at all. However she is really frail and underweight and she has old bruises on her legs.

It is thought that Edith may have been abused by her husband, Jack, who is 83 years old. Jack suffers from senile dementia and Parkinson's Disease. He is not housebound. The bus-stop is right outside the Middleton's house and Jack often gets on the bus and then gets lost.

The home help did refer the case to the divisional social services office six months ago. A social worker was allocated and became involved before this admission to hospital. It is known that Jack pushes Edith and sends her flying into things. Edith adamantly denies that Jack hits her but talks about him having been aggressive throughout the marriage because of his drinking habits. On one occasion Jack hit Edith causing her to fall down the stairs. She was pregnant at the time and miscarried twins. Jack does not drink now.

List of attenders

Chairperson

Mrs Parker, social worker

Mr Adams, consultant

Detective Inspector Johnson, police

Janice Burgess, home help

Nurse Baggeley, district nurse

Nurse West, state enrolled nurse on the ward

CASE CONFERENCE 1

ROLE: Chairperson

You are to chair the case conference on Edith Middleton, who is still in hospital at the present time. You have a list of people who are attending.

ROLE: Mrs Parker, social worker

You have been involved with this case for six months and have been visiting on a weekly basis. Edith welcomes you and enjoys the chance to talk but will not admit Jack hits her now. She only talks about his aggression in the past. You try to work with Jack in his lucid moments. The couple have refused to go to day centre either separately or together.

ROLE: Mr Adams, consultant

You have seen Edith once since she has been on the ward. You do not want to commit yourself to saying that her injuries were caused non-accidentally. However you do concede she may have been pushed. You remember vaguely that you have seen Edith before but have to keep referring to the medical notes.

ROLE: Detective Inspector Johnson, police

You are out for a conviction. You have been under pressure over the past few months and have not been getting results. Your boss is threatening to transfer you. You know nothing about senile dementia and you believe that Jack has assaulted Edith deliberately. You have interviewed both Edith and Jack. You think Jack could be made to confess his crime and then you could charge him with grievous bodily harm.

ROLE: Janice Burgess, home help

You have been involved with this couple for a couple of years. You go in twice a day (8.00 a.m. and 6.00 p.m.) to check if they are all right. You are sympathetic towards both of them. On the day of the accident they had both been fine in the morning. Your gut feeling tells you Jack does abuse Edith a lot and you have dreaded 'something awful happening'.

ROLE: Nurse Baggeley, district nurse

You go into the Middletons' home twice a week, once for Edith and once for Jack. You have regularly noticed bruises all over Edith's body but lots of old people have bruises because they are frail and always falling over. There are lots of people like Edith. You suppose Jack may have pushed her because you have often seen him in a bad mood. With the pressure of work you have not given it much thought.

ROLE: Nurse West, state enrolled nurse on the ward

You are a dedicated nurse who is very interested in working with older people. You have had to build up a relationship with Edith and you think she is on the point of telling you what really happened when she fell. From what she has said so far you are pretty sure Jack did push her.

CASE CONFERENCE 2

INFORMATION (to be given to all participants)

SUBJECT: *Betty Markham*
AGE: *71*

Betty, who is a widow, has lived in sheltered accommodation for the past four years. She has a son, John, who lives round the corner but rarely visits and a daughter, Val, who lives in Manchester and visits about once a month.

A few weeks ago there was a dramatic change in Betty's behaviour. She was very confused, disorientated in time and failed to recognise familiar people. She was often found walking round the corridor at 2.00 am. She was also frequently agitated. Betty became noticeably disinhibited and the content of her conversation was often inappropriately sexual. The caretaker in the sheltered housing complex became so concerned that he contacted the duty social worker.

Betty was examined by her general practitioner, the police surgeon and a psycho-geriatrician. It became apparent that Betty had been sexually abused by the man who lives in the bed-sit next door. Betty was admitted as an emergency to an old people's home for her own protection.

Betty has now been in the old people's home for two weeks and is agitating to go home. However, her son and daughter are pushing for her to remain in permanent care.

List of attenders
Chairperson
Mrs Mason, social worker
Mr Blades, principal, old people's home
Mrs Clark, home care organiser
Dr Sawyer, general practitioner
Miss Harrison, housing officer
Dr Pasmore, consultant psycho-geriatrician
Inspector Lambert, C.I.D.

CASE CONFERENCE 2

ROLE: Chairperson

You are to chair the case conference on Betty Markham, who is currently occupying a temporary bed in an old people's home. You have a list of people attending the case conference.

ROLE: Mrs Mason, social worker

You do not know Betty very well. You became involved when you were called out as duty social worker by the caretaker in the sheltered housing complex where Betty lives. You found Betty huddled in a corner very confused. You called in the general practitioner for investigation and eventually admitted Betty to an old people's home as an emergency. During the past two weeks you have visited Betty in the old people's home and are aware that Betty really wants to return home. However you have interviewed and received numerous phone calls from Betty's son and daughter who are determined that their mother should remain in permanent care.

ROLE: Mr Blades, principal, old people's home

You have known Betty for the past two weeks whilst she has been a resident in your home. You are able to tell the conference that she is a very confused lady who can become quite aggressive at times. She does get up in the middle of the night and has been found wandering around the home. It is very clear that Betty wants to return to her own bed-sit. Other information you can provide is that Betty is quite dependent. She needs to use a walking frame. She needs help with washing and bathing, but she can get to the toilet by herself.

ROLE: Mrs Clark, home care organiser

You have known Betty since her husband died ten years ago. You have been putting in full domiciliary services, i.e. warden three times a day and home help once a week. Your warden has been very worried about Betty for several months now. She has told you about the changes in Betty's behaviour and the fact that the man next door seems to visit Betty a great deal. Home care services are just about managing to maintain Betty at home, but you are concerned about her future. You can tell the conference that Betty also goes to luncheon clubs on a Tuesday and Wednesday.

ROLE: Dr Sawyer, general practitioner

You have been Betty's general practitioner for many years and you are able to argue that there has been a dramatic change in Betty's behaviour during the past few months. You were called out by the duty social worker to see Betty who was later examined by the police surgeon. You are not very keen on working with older people and tend to have the attitude that it really does not matter what has happened to her, especially as she is old and confused. The son and daughter have also been ringing you up asking if you can help get Betty into an old people's home permanently. You think this is a good idea and would be a good way of getting rid of Betty and the problem.

ROLE: Miss Harrison, housing officer

You have never been to a case conference before and you are very nervous, especially because of the nature of this case. You have been briefed by your supervisor. You are able to inform the conference that the man next door has been offered another bed-sit at the other end of the housing complex. You have interviewed this man and although he is denying that he has had sexual contact with Betty he is willing to move because he does not want any more allegations made against him.

ROLE: Dr. Pasmore, consultant psycho-geriatrician

You were asked to assess Betty after she had been admitted to the old people's home. You are actually under a lot of pressure at the moment and you are very behind with your paperwork. You have sent one of your standard letters to the social worker which says that Betty is starting to dement, is disorientated in time and place, she does not know who the Queen is, etc. You recommend that Betty needs a place in permanent care. You are not offering any services from hospital.

ROLE: Inspector Lambert, C.I.D.

You have a lot of sympathy with this case. You are able to present the evidence from the police surgeon. There was forensic evidence that Betty had been raped but the surgeon does not feel that this evidence would be enough to present in a Crown Court. You have interviewed Betty yourself and found that it was impossible to get a clear statement because she is mentally confused. You have also interviewed the neighbour next door who is old but not confused. He is denying any sexual contact with Betty. You are concerned for Betty's future safety but feel that the police cannot take any further action.

CASE CONFERENCE 3

INFORMATION (to be given to all participants)

SUBJECT: Byron McDonald
AGE: 65

Byron McDonald is West Indian and has lived in England for the past 30 years. He lives with his eldest daughter, Ella. His three other children have returned to live in Jamaica. His wife died many years ago. Byron has suffered several strokes which have left him paralysed on his left side and wheelchair bound. He is also a diabetic. He has refused to attend day hospital for any therapy and does not like having strangers in his house.

Ella works full-time as a nurse in a local hospital. She has always cared for her siblings both when their parents left them in Jamaica and when they came to England after their mother died. Ella feels very resentful that she now has to care for her father as she has no time for herself.

Five days ago Ella was very tired after working a difficult twelve hour shift. When she got home her father started moaning and shouting at her saying the house was a mess. Ella reached the end of her tether and physically attacked her father which resulted in severe bruising and cuts on his face and body. She has admitted this to the police but has asked to attend the care conference to explain her actions.

Byron was taken to the local Casualty Department by his social worker. After being examined he was returned home. A case conference has been convened to discuss his future care.

> *List of attenders*
> Chairperson
> Charlotte Banks, social worker
> Elaine Cook, home care warden
> Dr James, casualty doctor
> Mike Levitt, CID
> Sue Dashwood, community physiotherapist
> Jane Green, district nurse

Brother Wesley, volunteer from the local Pentecostal Church.

Ella McDonald, daughter of Byron.

CASE CONFERENCE 3

ROLE: Chairperson

You are to chair the case conference on Byron McDonald.
You have a list of people attending the conference.

ROLE: Charlotte Banks, social worker

Your department has just introduced as policy multi-disciplinary guidelines on working with abused older people. You are keen to follow the guidelines to the last letter. Five days ago you were contacted by the warden to tell you that your client, Byron McDonald, had severe bruising and cuts on his face and body. You had immediately dashed out and taken Byron to the hospital and informed the police. You have never managed to meet up with Byron's daughter and know little about her.

ROLE: Elaine Cook, warden

You go in to see Byron three times a day because his daughter works odd shifts at the hospital. Five days ago you went in early morning in order to get Byron up and to give him breakfast. As you dressed Byron you found severe bruising and cuts on his body. Byron said his daughter had hit him. You informed the social worker.

ROLE: Dr. James, casualty doctor

You examined Byron McDonald when he had been brought into the Casualty Department by his social worker. You can confirm that the injuries on his face and body had been inflicted non-accidentally. You had also found, some older bruising on Byron's legs.

ROLE: Mike Levitt, C.I.D.

You have interviewed both Byron McDonald and his daughter during the past few days. You feel sorry for the daughter as she is obviously under a lot of strain and gets little help from anybody. Byron has made a statement and wants his daughter 'to be taught a lesson'. You are very reluctant to take proceedings although you are aware of the new multi-disciplinary guidelines on working with abuse of older people.

ROLE: Sue Dashwood, community physiotherapist

You visit Byron twice a week because he refused to go to day hospital for any therapy. You are able to tell the conference that Byron is a very stubborn man who always wants his own way.

ROLE: Jane Green, district nurse

You come in to see Byron every day in order to give him his insulin injection. He is always very rude to you.

ROLE: Brother Wesley, volunteer from the local Pentecostal church

You have known Byron McDonald for the past 15 years. You take him to and from church three times a week. You speak highly of Byron but have little time for his daughter who does not attend church.

ROLE: Ella McDonald, daughter of Byron

You have asked to attend the case conference because you are fed-up with everyone being sympathetic towards your father and you want to have your say. You have never talked to anyone before about how you feel. You hate your father because he left you in Jamaica with an aunt and uncle. The uncle sexually abused you when you were twelve years old. You resent the fact that you have never been able to live your life as you would like because of having to look after your siblings and now your father.

CASE CONFERENCE 4

INFORMATION (to be given to all participants)

SUBJECT: Emma Harmer
AGE: 70

Emma Harmer lives in a two-bedroomed council flat with her daughter, Christine. Emma's husband, Rupert, died two years ago, and she has never got over this.

Christine is 40 years old and suffers with schizophrenia. She is prescribed medication, but from time to time refuses to take it. Christine has always lived with her parents and has never worked. She goes to a local day centre three times a week.

Five months ago, Emma suffered a stroke and was admitted to hospital. She regained her speech, but her left side is still slightly affected. She finds it difficult to move her arm, but her general mobility is improving. She attends day hospital twice a week (Monday and Thursday) and has physiotherapy whilst she is there. She also goes to a local authority day centre once a week (Friday).

Last Monday when Emma arrived at the day hospital she was extremely distressed. She was crying and holding her left arm to her chest. When staff helped Emma to take off her coat, she screamed with pain. Her left arm was bandaged up. When staff asked Emma what was the matter she showed them her arm, which was covered in cigarette burns and had an open cut approximately six inches long. Emma said her daughter had hurt her. Emma agreed to be taken to the Casualty Department and her social worker was contacted.

The elder abuse procedures were implemented and a full investigation followed. Today the case conference is due to take place.

> *List of attenders:*
>
> Chairperson
> Investigating officers: Emma's social worker
> Another social worker
> Casualty registrar
> General practitioner
> Day hospital nurse

Speech therapist

Physiotherapist

Local authority day centre worker

Christine's social worker

Christine's keyworker from day centre

Community psychiatric nurse

Police

APOLOGIES: Dr Anderson, Consultant from the
Stroke Unit

CASE CONFERENCE 4

ROLE: CHAIRPERSON

You are to chair this multidisciplinary case conference.
You have a list of people who are attending.

ROLE: EMMA'S SOCIAL WORKER

You have been involved with Emma since she was discharged
from hospital after her stroke. You visit once a week. You have
a lot of concerns about Emma. She has never come to terms with
the death of her husband, Rupert. She misses him terribly and
cries a lot about this. You are doing some bereavement counselling with Emma. You have picked up that Emma's daughter,
Christine, did not get on with her father, but you do not know
why. You know that Christine is schizophrenic and has a social
worker, but you have only spoken to him/her once at the
beginning of your involvement.

You were contacted by the staff in the day hospital to say that
Emma had been taken to Casualty. Since then you have been
involved as the Investigating Officer together with a colleague
from your team.

You have interviewed Emma on three occasions. At first all
she would say was that Christine had hurt her. Eventually she
admitted that Christine had burnt her with a cigarette and cut
her with a penknife. Emma made a statement to the police, but
has now withdrawn it, because she is frightened that Christine
will be sent to prison.

ROLE: INVESTIGATING OFFICER

You are a social worker who became involved in an elder abuse investigation when you were asked to go out with a colleague. You first met Emma when she was in the Casualty Department.

You have interviewed Emma on three occasions. At first all she would say was that Christine had hurt her. Eventually she admitted that Christine had burnt her with a cigarette and cut her with a penknife. Emma made a statement to the police, but has now withdrawn her statement, because she is frightened that Christine will be sent to prison,

You spoke to Christine in the hospital casualty department. She denied injuring her mother.

ROLE: NURSE IN THE DAY HOSPITAL

You were one of the staff who tended to Emma when she arrived in day hospital last Monday. You need to describe how distressed Emma was and that she said her daughter had 'hurt' her.

You have known Emma since she started coming to day hospital after her discharge from hospital. She attends on Mondays and Thursdays.

Emma is a very sad woman, who cries a lot. She talks non stop about her husband, Rupert, who is dead. She says little about her daughter, Christine, whom she describes as 'the sick girl'.

On several occasions Emma has come to day hospital with bruising on different parts of her face. She has always said that she has fallen when she has been trying to practice her walking. You seriously doubt this and are adamant during the conference that steps must be taken to find out what is really going on.

ROLE: SPEECH THERAPIST

You knew Emma when she was in hospital after her stroke. You saw her on a daily basis. She made excellent progress with her speech. You got to know her quite well. She talked a lot about her dead husband, Rupert. She told you stories about how kind he was to herself and their daughter. She described him as being 'gentle' and 'thoughtful'. She said Christine had never appreciated how good a father he was.

ROLE: PHYSIOTHERAPIST

You first got to know Emma when she was a patient on the stroke unit. You now see her twice a week in the day hospital when you give her physiotherapy. Emma's left arm is not progressing very well; she can do little with it. Her general mobility is improving.

You have talked to the day hospital staff about the various bruises you have found on Emma's arms and legs and have noted them down in your records. Emma has always said she has been 'clumsy' with herself.

You find Emma a depressing patient. She always wants to talk about the past and refuses to be drawn into conversation about her current situation. You have no information regarding Emma's daughter, Christine.

ROLE: LOCAL AUTHORITY DAY CENTRE WORKER

Emma has been coming to your day centre for the past two years. A social worker had done a one off visit after Emma's husband had died, referred her for a day centre place and then closed the case.

Emma has never really mixed very well in the centre. Other users think she is miserable because she cries a lot and only wants to talk about her dead husband. When she does talk about Rupert she goes on about how wonderfully kind and gentle he was.

She has only talked about her daughter, Christine, on one occasion. Emma was very upset at the time and kept saying that Christine was 'sick'. On another occasion, Emma came to the day centre with a black eye and said she had knocked her face when trying to brush her hair with her bad arm.

When Emma came to the day centre last Friday you noticed her arm was bandaged. When you asked Emma what had happened all she would say was that there had been a misunderstanding and it was not important.

You have never attended a case conference before and you feel sick at the thought of having to talk in a large group. Consequently, you are not very clear about the information you are giving.

ROLE: CASUALTY REGISTRAR

You examined Emma when she was brought into Casualty by the day hospital staff. Emma told you that her daughter had hurt her but would not elaborate on this. You can tell the conference that Emma had five cigarette burns on the top of her arm and a six inch cut on the lower part of the arm. You believe the injuries could have been two to three days old. The cut had not been attended to and had become infected.

ROLE: GENERAL PRACTITIONER

You really do not want to be at this case conference, because you could have been playing golf! Therefore, you are not very helpful to the conference.

You have known both Emma and Christine Harmer for many years. You also remember Emma's husband, Rupert. Emma is always ringing the surgery asking you to visit, but now you get the receptionist to deal with her.

You describe Christine as 'mad' and believe the 'do-gooders' can deal with her (i.e. social worker and day centre staff). You are aware that a community psychiatric nurse visits from time to time.

You will tell the conference that you remember many years ago Rupert asked you to visit Emma at home. He admitted to you that he had battered his wife because 'she hadn't been doing her duty'. You always found Rupert to be 'a pleasant chap'.

ROLE: SOCIAL WORKER FOR CHRISTINE

You have been involved with Christine for many years. You know a lot about her history, but are very worried about how much to disclose to the conference, because Christine has asked you to keep many things to yourself.

Christine has told you that she hated her father because he sexually abused her from when she was 12 years old. She believes that her mother knew what was happening and feels very resentful towards her. Christine feels very angry that her mother tells everyone what a wonderful person Rupert was. In fact he was physically violent towards Emma, who refused to have a sexual relationship with him after giving birth to Christine.

Christine is on medication but stops taking it when her mother really gets on her nerves. A community psychiatric nurse is involved but tends to rely on you for information.

You have talked to Christine about the recent incident. She says she has done nothing to hurt her mother and you believe her.

ROLE: COMMUNITY PSYCHIATRIC NURSE

You have known Christine for several years. You visit from time to time to check on her medication, but tend to liaise more with the social worker, who has a very good relationship with Christine. You are ambivalent about whether Christine would injure her mother.

ROLE: WORKER FROM MENTAL HEALTH DAY CENTRE

Christine has been attending your day centre for years. She is supposed to attend on Monday, Thursday and Friday, but her attendance can be erratic. Christine is well liked by both centre users and staff. She likes talking to people, but can have a temper if she does not get her own way. She talks openly about how fed up she gets with her mother, whom she describes as 'the moaner'. Christine does not talk about her father very much but you are sure that when he died Christine said she was glad because she hated him. Christine has told you about being accused of injuring her mother. She denies everything.

ROLE: POLICE OFFICERS

You have interviewed both Emma and Christine. Initially, Emma made a statement in which she said her daughter had got angry with her. She said Christine had burnt her left arm with a cigarette and then cut her with a penknife. The day after she withdrew her statement. You have visited Emma since but all she says is that she made a mistake. Christine had accidentally dropped her cigarette out of her mouth and then dropped the tray she was carrying. A knife fell from the tray and cut her. You do not believe this story. When you interviewed Christine all she would say was that she was not guilty; she had not hurt her mother. You did not believe her.

13 Simulation Exercises

The purpose of this exercise is to act out what could happen during the course of one working day once an allegation of abuse has been made by an individual to someone else. The hours of the working day are usually between 9.00 am. and 5.00 pm. The simulation exercise will normally last one hour.

There can be various scenarios, developments or situations which arise. It is important for participants in the exercise to be aware that there is no right or wrong outcome in the exercise. This is purely a learning experience which, it is hoped, will produce action and situations for further discussion.

Preparation

- Ideally, two leaders are needed to organize this exercise.
- A large room is needed with plenty of chairs. Two pairs of chairs need to be placed in the middle of the room, back to back.
- A large clock whose hands can be moved should be placed on a wall.
- Areas within the room need to be designated as worksites/locations and clearly signposted.
- Information for participants needs to be written/typed out and placed in envelopes before the exercise begins.

The Tasks

Leaders

1. To prepare the room.
2. To prepare the written information for participants.
3. To explain the objective of the exercise and the rules to the participants.
4. To give each participant a role and then an envelope.
5. To move the clock forward at appropriate intervals (this will be at the discretion of the leaders during the exercise and will depend on the progression of action).
6. To observe and listen to individuals/groups.
7. To stop the exercise at intervals so that all participants can listen to conversations, interviews, telephone conversations, etc.

Participants

1. To obtain a role.
2. To assimilate the information given.
3. To act out the situation.
4. To communicate with other participants as necessary.

Rules of the Exercise

1. Participants will need to communicate with each other as appropriate. They can do this in various ways e.g. in any of the settings, by visiting, interviewing, making a telephone call.
2. The four chairs in the centre of the room are two telephone lines. If a person wishes to telephone someone they need to sit on one of the chairs and shout out who they wish to speak to. That person then comes to sit next to the caller and the conversation takes place. If both lines are busy the caller has to wait until a line becomes free.
3. Everyone should proceed in a way which they think is appropriate to their role and the current situation, as it develops.

4. The leaders can listen in to any conversation at any time. They can ask everyone to freeze their interaction whilst some participants continue their dialogue.

5. In some exercises additional information may be available from the leaders.

Feedback

After the simulation exercise has taken place participants need to discuss what has happened. It is useful for participants to split into groups (not the same group in which they have been role playing) and analyse critically the actions/procedures. The group will then feed back into the large group.

SIMULATION EXERCISE 1

Setting the scene: information for the leaders only

The victim is Hilda Baimbridge, aged 75 years. She has been sexually abused by her son, Victor, aged 45 years, for many years. Six weeks ago Victor came out of prison on parole. He had been serving a three year prison sentence after raping a young woman.

The following roles need to be allocated:

Hilda Baimbridge, aged 75 years
Victor Baimbridge, aged 45 years, son of Hilda
Home help
Home care organizer
Duty social worker, level 1
Duty social worker, level 2
Duty principal social worker
Probation officer
General practitioner
District nurse
Two police persons from C.I.D.
Police surgeon

Locations which need to be sited in the room:

>Home of Hilda
>Home help office
>Social services office
>Probation office
>General practitioner's surgery
>Community health clinic
>Police station

Information to be given to participants:

ROLE: Hilda Baimbridge (75 years)

You are at home and your home help has arrived. You have just told her that your son Victor, aged 45, has been forcing you to have sex with him since he came out of prison six weeks ago. This has happened before but you have never told anybody about it. Victor is out on parole having been in prison for several years after raping a young woman. You love Victor dearly but he has started being physically violent towards you and you feel you cannot go on like this.

ROLE: Victor Baimbridge (aged 45 years) son of Hilda

You have been out of prison for six weeks and are on parole. You were sent down for three years after raping a 25-year-old woman. You have seen your probation officer several times but have missed a recent appointment. This morning you are on your way to the probation office. Unknown to anyone else you have been forcing your mother, with whom you live, to have sex for many years, but since coming out of prison this has become more frequent. Your previous girlfriend married someone else while you were in prison.

ROLE: Home help

Today you are due to spend four hours working in the home of Hilda Baimbridge, aged 75 years, whom you have known for about a year. Hilda lives with her son Victor. When you arrived this morning you found that Hilda was very upset. She then told you that Victor has been forcing her to have sex with him and this has been going on ever since he came out of prison six weeks

155

ago. Hilda is now very frightened because Victor is becoming violent. She has shown you blood stains on the sheets and bruises on her body. You believe Hilda and immediately telephone your home care organizer to find out what to do next.

ROLE: Home care organizer

You are just about to go out of the office to do some visits when you get a telephone call from one of your home helps. She says her client, Hilda Baimbridge, has been forced to have sex with her son Victor. She has asked you what she should do now. You agree to contact the duty social worker.

ROLE: Duty social worker, level 1

You take a phone call from a home care organizer. She tells you that one of her home helps is with a 75-year-old client, Hilda Baimbridge, who has said that her son has forced her to have sex with him.

ROLE: Duty social worker, level 2

You are sitting on the duty desk writing up some of your own case files. You are on duty with a level 1 worker who is taking a referral about a possible sexual abuse case involving a 75-year-old woman and her son.

ROLE: Duty principal social worker

This morning you are on duty and you have to attend a management team meeting. You have told your duty team which consists of a level 1 and a level 2 worker that you do not want to be disturbed unless absolutely necessary.

ROLE: Probation officer

Your client is Victor Baimbridge, aged 45 years, who is on parole. He was sent down for three years after raping a 25-year-old woman. You have seen Victor several times during the past six weeks but have not got to know him very well. This morning you are in your office seeing other clients.

ROLE: General practitioner

You have known 75-year-old Hilda Baimbridge and her son Victor for as long as you can remember. You have seen quite a lot of Hilda recently because she has been ringing the surgery asking you to visit. There has been no particular change in Hilda's health recently. She suffers from arthritis and her mobility is restricted. Hilda has always been a very independent woman but on your last couple of visits she has asked you if she can go into hospital 'for a rest'. You seem to remember that the district nurse has been going on about something in relation to Hilda Baimbridge but you cannot recall exactly what she said.

ROLE: District nurse

You visit Hilda Baimbridge once a week to give her a bath. During the past six weeks you have noticed a change in Hilda. She has become nervous and edgy. You have noticed some bruises on Hilda's arms and on the inside of her thighs. When you asked Hilda about the bruises, she said she kept falling over and maybe it is time she thought about going somewhere to be looked after like in an old people's home. You are also concerned because Hilda's son, Victor, has tried to stop you coming to bath his mother. You have voiced your concerns to the general practitioner.

ROLE: Two detectives in C.I.D.

You are working in your office this morning trying to catch up on paperwork.

ROLE: Police surgeon

You are on call for anything which may come up during the course of the day.

SIMULATION EXERCISE 2

Setting the scene: information for the leaders only

The victim is 69-year-old Albert. He lives alone and is abused by his only daughter, Joan, who is married to an alcoholic.

The following roles need to be allocated:

Albert, aged 69 years

Joan, Albert's daughter

Neighbour

Community psychiatric nurse

General practitioner

Day centre staff x 2

Duty social work team comprising:

social work assistant, senior social worker and team leader

Receptionist (optional)

C.I.D. officers x 2

Hospital casualty staff—doctor, sister, nurse(s)

Locations which need to be sited in the room:

Day centre in old people's home

Joan's house

Neighbour's house

Community psychiatric nurse's office in clinic

General practitioner's surgery

Social services area office

Police car

Casualty Department in a city hospital

Information to be given to participants:

ROLE: Albert (aged 69 years)

You suffer from severe depression and have attempted suicide on several occasions. You miss your wife, Ethel, who died of cancer five years ago. You have one daughter, Joan, who only visits you when she needs money. Last night she came to see you at 7 o'clock and demanded £100 to pay her gas and electricity bills. When you refused to give her any money she became very angry. She hit you with your own walking stick and her cigarette fell out of her mouth onto your left hand leaving a burn mark. Today you are at the day centre which you normally enjoy. However, you are feeling very upset this morning. You tell the day centre staff that you cannot remember how you got the bruising on your face or the burn mark on your hand.

ROLE: Joan

You are married to Harry and have three children. Harry has a drink problem and there is never enough money to pay the bills or buy clothes for the children. You usually manage to get money out of your dad, Albert, but last night he refused to help you. You got very angry. You hit him with his walking stick and whilst you were doing this your cigarette dropped out of your mouth onto his left hand. You are at home this morning.

ROLE: Neighbour

You live next door to Albert who is aged 69 and lives alone. Last night at about 7 o'clock you heard shouting and what seemed like hitting. This has happened before but seemed much worse last night. You heard Albert cry 'stop it, stop it'. Your husband would not let you phone the police and told you to mind your own business. You cannot stop thinking about what happened and you decide to make an anonymous phone call to the Social Services Department this morning.

ROLE: Community psychiatric nurse

You have been visiting Albert for several years now. He is always depressed. He talks to you about his wife, Ethel, who died five years ago and whom he misses very much. He says little about his only daughter, Joan, and when you try to bring her into the conversation he always changes the subject.

ROLE: General practitioner

You do not know much about Albert. In fact you cannot remember the last time you saw him. You just sign his prescriptions for anti-depressants every month.

ROLE: Day centre staff x 2

Albert has arrived at day centre this morning very weepy. You know he gets depressed but he has never been like this before. You notice he has got bruising on his cheek and around one of his eyes. There is also a burn mark on his left hand. He says he cannot remember how he got the bruising or the burn.

ROLE: Duty social work team in a busy social services area office comprising team leader, senior social worker and social work assistant.

It is a busy Friday morning. There are three people waiting in the reception area and two phone calls to return. The reception-ist then receives an anonymous phone call. The caller says she is a neighbour and wants to report an incident last night. The call is passed to the social work assistant.

ROLE: C.I.D. Officers x 2

You are out on visits but may be contacted by phone if necessary.

ROLE: Hospital casualty staff—doctor, sister, nurse(s)

You are working in a busy Accident and Emergency Department in a large city hospital.

Additional Information (to be held by the leaders)

The following additional information is available on miscella-neous papers which are held in the social services area office.

There has been previous social work involvement with Albert and his wife.

Five years ago a social work assistant was involved with Albert's wife when she was terminally ill. Practical help had been given to the couple and the occupational therapist had been involved in providing various aids.

The social work assistant remained involved with Albert for about six months after his wife's death. An application was made to a day centre and once Albert was successful in obtaining a place the case was closed.

There have been various referrals during the past three years about Albert's depression from various people, e.g. day centre staff, a neighbour etc. The case has not been allocated but a community psychiatric nurse has become involved. The most recent referral was about six months ago when the community psychiatric nurse reported that she was concerned about odd bruising on Albert's face.

SIMULATION EXERCISE 3

Setting the scene: information for the leaders only.

The victim is Agnes, aged 86, who lives alone. Agnes is slightly forgetful and becomes confused sometimes. The people involved with her believe she is starting to dement. Local youths are coming into her house during the evenings when they know no-one will be there and they are abusing her physically and financially. Nobody believes Agnes when she says people come into her house.

The following roles need to be allocated

Agnes, aged 86 years
Hospital staff in Accident and Emergency Department
in a city hospital:
Doctor, sister, nurse and student nurse
Consultant psycho-geriatrician
Hospital social worker
Area social worker
Home care staff:
Home care organizer, warden, home help
Day centre staff
Care assistants in old people's home
Police officers x 2

Locations which need to be sited in the room:

Accident and Emergency Department, city hospital
Social Work Department in the hospital
Psycho-geriatrician's office
Area social services office
Home help office
Day centre
Old people's home
Police station

Information to be given to participants:

ROLE: Agnes (aged 86 years)

You rang for an ambulance late last night after you had been attacked by a gang of youths in your own house. Sometimes you find it difficult to remember what has just happened although you can remember things that happened to you years ago. This morning you have woken up and found yourself in the Casualty Department of a large hospital. You can remember ringing for the ambulance because your arm hurts. You know that young people keep coming into your house every night. You keep telling everyone that people come into your house at night but everyone just seems to laugh at you. You know that these young people ask for money and hit you if you do not give them your pension.

ROLE: Hospital casualty staff—doctor, sister, nurse, student nurse

Agnes came into the Casualty Department late last night after she had called for an ambulance. Her right arm is broken. She presents as being very confused and is probably suffering from senile dementia. She cannot remember very much about what happened last night. She keeps repeating that people come into her house late at night. She also keeps saying that she is losing money. All she remembers about last night is that her arm hurt and that she telephoned for an ambulance.

ROLE: Consultant psycho-geriatrician

You need to be on call. You may be asked to see a woman in casualty.

ROLE: Hospital social worker

A referral has come through from the Casualty Department. You have been asked to see an 86-year-old woman, Agnes, who came to the Casualty Department in an ambulance late last night. She has a broken arm. She has spent the night in the transit ward of the Casualty Department.

ROLE: Area social worker

The case of Agnes is allocated to you but you have been meaning to close it for sometime. Initially you were involved in an application for day centre and since then have arranged short term care, then respite care in an old people's home for Agnes. Agnes's mental state has deteriorated and you believe she is suffering from senile dementia. Last time you saw her she was going on about the fact that people come in and out of her house during the night.

ROLE: Home care staff—home care organizer, warden, home help

Eighty-six year-old Agnes has been known to the service for several years. She lives alone and is visited by the warden three times a day and the home help once a week.

ROLE: Day centre staff

Agnes has been attending day centre for a couple of years now. She is a very pleasant lady and is well liked both by staff and people who attend the day centre. Recently, however, she has started to become forgetful and seems confused. The social worker has arranged some short term care and now Agnes is having regular respite care in the old people's home to which the day centre is attached.

ROLE: Care staff in the old people's home

Agnes started coming in for short term care, because her mental condition was deteriorating, she is now in receipt of regular respite care. She also attends the day centre which is attached to the old people's home. She is a very pleasant woman and is well liked by staff and residents. However she seems to be getting more confused and talks a great deal about the people who come in and out of her house at night. Nobody actually believes Agnes.

ROLE: Police officers x 2

You are on duty in the police station.

14 Scenarios

This final chapter contains a number of scenarios which may be used in different ways. I have found that many learners like to have case studies to discuss in pairs or groups. Alternatively, trainers may wish to use the material for some of the exercises presented in Chapters 6, 7 and 8. The scenarios could also be expanded and developed for larger exercises such as the case conference.

Mr A is an 83-year-old man who is cared for by his 82-year-old wife. He suffers from Alzheimer's Disease, which is severe. He is doubly incontinent, has prostate problems and is violent. Mrs A cannot come to terms with the change in her husband's personality. She is finding it very difficult to cope with the situation and often threatens to commit suicide herself.

Mrs E is 88 years old and has had a stroke. She is slightly handicapped and very depressed about her health. She has lived with her 60-year-old unmarried son since her husband died some years ago. The son had retired early so he could enjoy his hobbies, especially walking outdoors. He had always been pampered by his mother and cannot cope with the changes brought about by her stroke. He sees her illness as a weakness.

Mrs J is 68 years old and cannot do anything for herself. She is mentally infirm, doubly incontinent and tends to wander off. She is cared for by her husband, H, who is also in his sixties. H is very resentful that he cannot enjoy his retirement. He had worked hard for many years and was looking forward to taking life easy.

Mrs D is a frail but mentally sound 81-year-old black woman. Her 36-year-old son, T, suffers from schizophrenia and he had abused his father before he died. Mrs D lives in one room of a large house. Her son has cut off her contact with others, for example the home help, because people had started asking about his mother's bruises. As well as hitting her, he deprived her of food and eats the meals prepared for his mother by the warden.

Mrs S has been abused by her son for eight years, since she was 64 years old. At that time it was thought she was in the early stages of dementia but the new social worker now believes that the symptoms are of depression rather than dementia. Her 42-year-old son has learning disabilities. Mother and son were devoted to each other and used to go on drinking bouts together. However, the son started physically abusing his mother and sister and deprived them of food and heating. Mrs S is now severely disorientated and stays in bed all the time.

Mr R is in his seventies and has looked after his wife, who suffered from senile dementia, until she was admitted to permanent care. Mr and Mrs R had always had one of their sons living with them. This son is now in his thirties, slightly deformed with a hump back, and he has a drink problem. Mr and Mrs R had always provided financially for their son. Once Mrs R was in permanent care, Mr R's income was severely reduced (he lost his wife's pension, attendance allowance etc.). It was then that his son started beating him up as he would not hand over his pension. He has now forced his father to put his savings in a joint bank account.

Mr D is 77 years old and severely physically handicapped. As part of this handicap he cannot communicate at all. He lives with two middle aged men who are both violent and have served prison sentences for violent crimes (grievous bodily harm etc.). They have a lot of financial problems and the social worker believes that they need Mr D because he gets a war pension and they receive his attendance allowance. They use both for their own purposes.

Mr W is an extremely difficult man of 80 years whom nobody likes because he is physically violent and verbally abusive to everyone. He is mentally sound but has been housebound following a hip replacement. He also suffers from eczema and a stomach complaint. He is cared for by his daughter who admits hitting him. She has been depressed since her husband's recent death and her mobility is restricted due to swollen arthritic knees. She has been waiting for surgery for some time.

Seventy year old Mrs D has referred herself to the social services department, saying that her husband abuses her physically and mentally when he drinks, which she claims he does from early in the morning every day. Mr D has admitted drinking in moderation but firmly denies he has a drink problem. Mrs D has suffered a stroke and is housebound. She also suffers from angina and diabetes.

Mrs L has been heavily dependent on tranquillizers for many years but now she has suddenly been taken off them completely at the age of 87. She has become very forgetful and is frightened to go out on her own. She lives with her son who has a withered arm and has never worked. Mrs L is suffering from general neglect, lack of food and verbal abuse.

Mrs S is 70 years old and mentally sound. She has suffered a stroke and developed leukemia. Her husband, who is mentally ill, physically hits her all over her body and throws things at her. Mrs S says her husband cannot help what he does to her. The couple have become very isolated as Mrs S's family have stopped having anything to do with her because of her husband.

Mrs W who lives alone has been referred to the home care service for help with the administration of her medication. She is 79 years old, suffering from senile dementia and is physically weak. The home help is suspicious that the next door neighbour is interfering with the medication and is physically abusing Mrs W on a regular basis.

Mrs D is a housebound 82-year-old who is slightly confused. She is abused financially by her son, M, who is in his mid forties employed and has a drink problem. The warden has found a letter from the Housing Department which states that Mrs D has rent arrears amounting to £1000. M has his mother's pension and attendance allowance book. He is refusing to leave money for the wardens to buy food.

Mrs L is 77 years old and lives on her own. She is mobile, sometimes forgetful but not confused. She suffers from depression, angina and arthritis of the spine. She has been referred by a neighbour to the social services department. The neighbour has said that Mrs L's daughter has taken her pension book from her and is not giving her enough money to live on.

Mrs A is 90 years old and previously was cared for by her daughter, who died. Her son has now become involved. He cashes her pension and takes all the money, supposedly to pay bills. He never buys any food or gives Mrs A any money. Mrs A presents as being frail, nearly blind, deaf, anaemic and suffers with head lice. There is never any food in the house. The warden is using her own money to buy food.

Mrs M has been an alcoholic for many years. She is now 60 years old and has had half her liver removed, suffered brain damage through the alcohol abuse, is incontinent and housebound. She has no friends who visit her and she is abused physically, verbally and financially by her son who lives with her.

Mr I is a 70-year-old West Indian man who is mentally ill. He lives alone and is deaf which makes him an easy target for youths to steal money from him. Various local school children, all male between the ages of 13 and 18 years, frequently go into Mr I's house. They have started demanding money from him. Windows have been smashed on several occasions.

Mrs J, aged 88 years is physically abused by her son, who suffers from epilepsy. Mr J had been off work for a long time and now he has been told that he is fit again but he does not want to return to work. His mother is overweight and catheterized. He abuses her by hitting and kicking her. He has now hit her over the head with a stick.

Eighty-year-old Mrs E suffers from senile dementia and arthritis. The warden has reported to the home care organizer that she has seen Mrs E being attacked by her husband, which has resulted in scratches and bruising on her arms.

Mrs R is 70 years old, a stroke victim and is quite confused. She lives with and is physically abused by her husband who has also suffered a stroke. He has little patience with his wife and tends to walk too fast in the street, causing her to fall over regularly. He has also been hitting her at home.

Miss A has not been well for years. She suffers from gynaecological problems and breast cancer and has recently undergone surgery on her bowel. Three years ago she gave up her job to care for her 80-year-old mother who is confused and diabetic. Since then she has abused her mother both physically and financially. Mrs A is neglected by her daughter and as a result lives in extremely poor conditions.

Seventy-seven-year-old Mrs J lives with her 19-year-old grandson. Mrs J has a history of psychiatric problems and is very depressed. She is mobile and can get out of the house. She seems to enjoy having her grandson around. Mrs J is abused physically and financially by both her daughter and her grandson. She is neglected physically. There is never any food in the house because the grandson eats what food there is and takes her money. The daughter takes her pension and the attendance allowance. Items such as bedding also disappear regularly from the house.

Mrs O is 69 years old and 13 years younger than her husband, who has married for the second time. Mrs O has suffered a stroke which has immobilized her and left her with limited speech. Her husband is blind, suffers from depression (he has attempted suicide on several occasions) and finds it increasingly difficult to care for his wife. He abuses her physically, emotionally and financially. He has now arranged to put her into care but has not told his wife this.

Two years ago 87-year-old Mrs M moved to live with her 82-year-old friend, Mrs J, and her mentally ill son. She has never given up her own flat. Mrs M is said to be backward. She cannot read or write and suffers from anaemia, arthritis and agoraphobia. A home help has been involved with both Mrs M and Mrs J for several years. She deals with,both pensions and says that £20 disappears every week from Mrs M's money. Mrs J had always had difficulties with her money previous to living with Mrs M but now she is able to pay all her bills and keep her son. She emotionally abuses Mrs M by continually putting pressure on her to remain living with her and her son.

Mr E is a one arm amputee who is mentally and financially abused by his daughter who lives a few doors away. He is left in a cot bed all day and is completely isolated because his television and radio have been taken away. The district nurse has suggested Mr E should be got up but the daughter says he will fall. The nurse has offered to strap him safely into a chair but again this has been rejected.

The police became involved with 66-year-old Mr F when his wallet, containing £350, went missing. Mr F is housebound and totally isolated due to heart trouble and trouble with one leg which causes him to use crutches. It is well known that he is visited regularly by young men in their twenties. The home help suspects that the young men are taking Mr F's money.

Both Mr and Mrs E, who are in their eighties are confused. The warden has started noticing bruising on Mrs E. She has now been missing on two occasions and Mr E did not even notice she had gone. The neighbour has reported to social services that she has heard Mr E hitting his wife and that he often throws her out of the house. They have both started to attend day centre, but last week Mr E hit Mrs E in front of the day centre staff. The general practitioner was asked to visit and it came to light that Mrs E 'had had a good pasting' the night before and was badly bruised.

Sixty-four-year-old Mrs G was admitted to hospital with a broken leg, finger-tip bruising and hypothermia. She seemed very frail and neglected. She lives with her husband who is partially sighted and her daughter, who is diabetic. Mrs G and her daughter admitted that Mr G had kicked his wife after she had fallen. Neither of them wanted the matter taken further and the family refused entry to any services offered, including the district nurse who is supposed to dress Mrs G's leg ulcers.

Mr E has been physically violent towards his wife throughout their marriage and this has continued whilst the couple are in their eighties. He is a large man who suffers from dementia. He is particularly violent in the mornings when he does not want to get up or be dressed. Recently Mrs E was found crying at the end of the street after Mr E had hit her and thrown her out. Mrs E talks about the ongoing abuse but refuses to let her husband go into care.

Two youths, aged 12 and 16 years, are taking advantage of a lonely 73-year-old woman. Mrs D suffers from mild dementia, diabetes and is an alcoholic. The youths drink socially with Mrs D. After they have got drunk together they steal money and food from Mrs D and regularly break into the gas and electric meters and wreck her bungalow.

Seventy-nine-year-old Mrs E is mentally alert but quite handicapped physically. She is abused by her son, W, verbally, emotionally and financially. Both the social worker and home help have heard W screaming at and threatening Mrs E. He keeps her pension book and places large grocery orders on behalf of his mother which he then takes to his own home.

Mr P, aged 81, seemed to give up on life when his wife died eight years ago. He is very frail and suffers from high blood pressure. He is financially abused by a neighbour who is in her thirties, unemployed, and lives a few streets away. The home help keeps reporting that Mr P is short of money. Six weeks ago Mr P's bank book disappeared. It has now reappeared and the home help has seen that £700 has been taken out over a few weeks.

Seventy-year-old Mr E has suffered a stroke which has affected his balance and he is also diabetic. His daughter has remarried and has a young baby. She never leaves Mr E enough money. She says she leaves between £17 and £20 a week but the home help can never find it. Often there is never any food in the house and if the daughter does bring any food it is inappropriate for a diabetic.

Mentally handicapped Mrs W is 70 years old and lives on her own. She is abused by her son who is in his fifties. She has recently received a community care grant which the son has cashed and put towards buying a second hand car. He regularly spends her pension money.

Seventy-four-year-old Mr D has suffered a left hemiparesis and was cared for by his wife who has a history of psychiatric and psychological problems. Mrs D is physically abusing her husband by starving him.

Mr and Mrs T have always had a stormy marriage. Mr T is violent and his wife has left the marital home several times even in recent years. Mrs T is mentally sound and mobile but suffers from pernicious anaemia and heart trouble. Mr T is confused and has long spells of paranoia. There are also periods when he is not mobile. Mr T has violent outbursts during which time his wife has to lock herself away.

Mrs L is 79 years old and has previously lived by herself but during the past year she has gone to live with her son, daughter-in-law and four children. She is suffering from Parkinson's Disease and is an insulin dependant diabetic. The social worker became involved with Mrs L's son and family when there were allegations that Mr L was abusing his daughters. The social worker reported that 'Mrs L's pension and attendance allowance seems to be fully incorporated into the family's budget'. Concerns are raised now that Mrs L has come into hospital and is complaining of chest pains. She says her daughter-in-law has pushed her onto her walking frame. She does not want to return home.

Ninety-eight-year-old Mrs N is terminally ill with cancer and has been admitted to hospital. She has nothing to do with her daughter, but her granddaughter has taken £400 in cash from her 'in case something happens'. There are rent arrears, an outstanding electricity bill and the poll tax needs to be paid. The granddaughter is refusing to pay the bills and expecting the hospital 'to sort things out'.

Asian Mrs K lives in a sparsely furnished attic with a one-bar electric fire as the only source of heating. Her extended family live downstairs in a very comfortably furnished house. Mrs K has suffered several strokes and is immobile. She has recently been visited by the occupational therapist who is concerned that she is being neglected by the rest of her family and is concerned that she has been financially abused.

Bibliography

Age Concern (1986) *The Law and Vulnerable Elderly People.* London: Age Concern.

Association of Directors of Social Services (1991) *Adults at risk.* Lancaster: ADSS.

August, P. (1987) 'Threats to harm elderly people must always be taken seriously', *Social Work Today* 10th August, 14–15.

B.A.S.W. (1990) *Abuse of Elderly People—Guidelines for Action.* Birmingham: B.A.S.W.

Baker, A.A. (1975) 'Granny Battering', *Modern Geriatrics, 5,* (8), 20–24.

Bedford Social Services Department (1989) *The abuse of elderly people: Summary of workshop and projects 1987–1988.* London: Bedfordshire County Council

Bennett, G. (April 1990) 'Action on elder abuse in the '90s: New definition will help', *Geriatric Medicine, 20,* (4), 53–54.

Bennett, G. (May 1990) 'Shifting emphasis from abused to abuser'. *Geriatric Medicine* 20 (5), 45–47.

Bennett, G. (July 1990) 'Assessing abuse in the elderly'. *Geriatric Medicine* 20 (7), 49–51.

Bennett, G. (August 1990) 'Getting through to the abused elderly'. *Geriatric Medicine* 20 (8), 25–26.

Bennett, G. (October 1990) 'Abuse of the elderly: Prevention and Legislation'. *Geriatric Medicine* 20 (10), 55–60.

Bennett, G. and Kingston, P. (1993) *Elder abuse: concepts, ideas and interventions.* London: Chapman and Hall.

Bexley, London Borough of (1988) *Abuse of elderly people: Recognising the problem.* Papers 1–3. London: Borough of Bexley.

Bookin, D. and Dunkle, E.R. (January 1985) 'Elder Abuse: Issues for the practitioner'. *Social Casework: The Journal of Contemporary Social Work,* 3–12.

Browne, Dr. K.D. (1989) 'Family violence: Spouse and elder abuse', in Howells, K. and Hollin, C. (eds) *Clinical Approaches to Violence.* London: John Wiley and Sons.

Burston, G.R. (September 1975).'Granny Battering' *British Medical Journal* 3, 592–593.

Burston, G.R. (May 1977) 'Do your elderly patients live in fear of being battered?' *Modern Geriatrics* 7 (5), 54–55.

Cloke, C (1983) *Old Age Abuse in the Domestic Setting—a Review.* London: Age Concern.

Clough, R. (1988) 'Danger look out for abuse', *Care Weekly*, 29th January.

Clough, R. (unpublished) *Scandals in residential care*. Paper prepared for the Wagner Committee.

Counsel and Care (1991) *Not such private places*. London: Counsel and care.

Crossroads Care (May 1990) *Caring for Carers—a Nationwide Survey*. London: Monica Hart Press and Public Relations.

Decalmer, P. and Glendenning, F. (1993) *The mistreatment of elderly people*. London: Sage.

Eastman, M. (1984a) *Old Age Abuse*. London: Age Concern.

Eastman, M. (February 1984b) 'At worst just picking up the pieces'. *Community Care*, 20–22.

Eastman, M. (October 1988) 'Granny Abuse'. *Community Outlook*, 15–16.

Eastman, M. (1989) 'Studying Old Age Abuse'. In J. Archer and K.D. Browne (eds) *Human Aggression: Naturalistic Approaches*. London: Routledge.

Eastman, M. (1994) *Old age abuse* 2. London: Chapman and Hall.

Eastman, M. and Sutton, M. (1982) 'Granny Battering', *Geriatric Medicine*, 12, (11), 11–15.

Enfield Social Services Department (1993) *Notes of Guidance (Practice and Procedure)*. London: Borough of Enfield.

Garrett, G. (August 1986) 'Old age abuse by carers', *The Professional Nurse*, 304–305.

Gelles, R.J. and Cornell, C.P. (1985) *Intimate violence in families*. Beverley Hills, CA: Sage.

Gibbs, J., Evans, M. and Rodway, S. (1987) *Report of Inquiry into Nye Bevan Lodge*. London: Southwark Social Services Department.

Gostin, L, (1983) *A Practical Guide to Mental Health Law*. London: MIND.

Halliley, M. (1987) 'A licence to profit from abuse of the elderly', *The Listener*, 8th October.

Hickey, T. and Douglass, R.L. (1981) 'Neglect and Abuse of older family members: Professionals' perspectives and case experiences', *The Gerontologist*, 21, (2), 171–176.

Hildrew, M.A. (1991) 'New age problems', *Social Work Today*, 22, (49), 15–17.

Hocking, E.D. (1988) 'Miscare—a form of abuse in the elderly', *Update*, 15th May, 2411–2419.

Holt, M.G. (1993) 'Elder sexual abuse in Britain: preliminary findings', *Journal of Elder Abuse and Neglect*, 5, No.2, 63–71.

Homer, A.C. and Gilleard, C. (1990) 'Abuse of elderly people by their carers', *British Medical Journal*, 301, 1359–1362.

Homer, A.C. and Kingston, P. (1992) 'Screening by nurse practitioners could prevent elder abuse', *Care of the Elderly*, 220–222.

Hudson M.F. (1989) 'Analysis of the concepts of elder mistreatment: abuse and neglect', *Journal of Elder Abuse and Neglect*, 1, (1), 5–25.

Judge, K. and Sinclair, I. (1986) *Residential care for the elderly*. London: HMSO.

Kent Social Services Department (1987) *Practice guidelines for dealing with elder abuse*. Maidstone: Kent County Council.

Kinderknecht, C.H. (Spring 1986) 'In home social work with abused or neglected elderly: an experiential guide to assessment and treatment', *Journal of Gerontological Social Work*, 9, (3), 29–42.

Knight, B. (April 1983) 'Geriatric Homicide—or the Darby and Joan Syndrome', *Geriatric Medicine*, 13, (4), 297–299.

Law Commission (1991) *Mentally Incapacitiated Adults and Decision Making: An Overview. Consultation paper No 119*. London: HMSO.

Law Commission (1993a) *Mentally incapacitated adults and decision-making: a new jurisdiction. Consultation paper No 128*. London: HMSO.

Law Commission (1993b) *Mentally incapacitated adults and decision-making: medical treatment and research. Consultation paper No 129*. London: HMSO.

Law Commission (1993c) *Mentally incapacitated and other vulnerable adults. Public law protection. Consultation paper No 130*. London: HMSO.

McCreadie, C. (1991) *Elder abuse: an exploratory study*. London: Age Concern. Institute of Gerontology.

McCreadie, C. (1993) *Elder abuse: new findings and policy guidelines*. London: Age Concern. Institute of Gerontology.

McCreadie, C. and Tinker, A. (1993) 'Abuse of elderly people in the domestic setting: a U.K. perspective', *Age and Ageing*, 22, 65–69.

National Institute of Social Work (1988) *Residential care: a positive choice*. London: NISW.

Ogg, J. and Bennett, G. (February 1992) 'Screening for elder abuse in the Community', *Geriatric Medicine*, Feb, 63–67.

Ogg, J. and Bennett, G. (October 1992) 'Elder abuse in Britain', *British Medical Journal*, 305, 998–999

Ogg, J. and Munn-Giddings, C. (1993) 'Researching elder abuse', *Ageing and Society*, 13, 389–413.

Penhale, B. (1993) 'The abuse of elderly people: considerations for practice', *British Journal of Social Work*, 23(2), 95–112.

Phillipson, C. and Biggs, S. (1992) *Understanding elder abuse: a training manual for helping professionals*. London: Longman.

Pillemer, K. and Finkelhor, D. (1988) 'The prevalence of elder abuse: A random sample survey', *The Gerontologist, 28,* (1), 51–57.

Piper, M. (1986) *Violence in the elderly* (unpublished).

Poertner, J. (Spring 1986) 'Estimating the incidence of abused older persons', *Journal of Gerontologial Social Work, 9,* (3), 3–15.

Pritchard, J.H. (1989) 'Confronting the taboo of the abuse of elderly people', *Social Work Today,* 5th October, 12–13.

Pritchard, J.H. (1990a) 'Old and Abused', *Social Work Today,* 15th February, 22–23.

Pritchard, J.H. (1990b) 'Charting the Hits', *Care Weekly,* 19th October, 10–11.

Pritchard, J.H. (February 1991a) 'Identifying Abuse', *Community Outlook, 1,* (2), 19–20.

Pritchard, J.H. (1991b) 'Sufferers in Silence', *Care Weekly,* 9th August, 10–11.

Pritchard, J.H. (1993a) 'Dispelling some myths', *Journal of Elder Abuse and Neglect, 5,* No.2, 27–35.

Pritchard, J.H. (1993b) 'Gang warfare', *Community Care, 8th July,* 22–23.

Public Trust Office (April 1988) *Handbook for Receivers.* London: Public Trust Office.

Public Trust Office (November 1989) *Procedure notes and forms on the work of the Court of Protection and Protection Division.* London: Public Trust Office.

Public Trust Office (July 1990) *Enduring Powers of Attorney.* London: Public Trust Office.

Ramsey-Klawsnik, H. (1991) 'Elder sexual abuse: preliminary findings', *Journal of Elder Abuse and Neglect, 3,* No.3, 73–90.

Rathbone-McCuan, E. (May 1980) 'Elderly victims of family violence and neglect', *Social Casework: The Journal of Contemporary Social Work,* 296–304.

Riley, P. (1989) *'Professional dilemmas in elder abuse'* (unpublished).

Royal College of Nursing (1991) *Guidelines for Nurses—Abuse and Older People.* London: Royal College of Nursing.

Sanford, J.R.A. (1975) 'Tolerance of debility in elderly dependants by supporters at home: its significance for hospital practice', *British Medical Journal,* 23rd August, 471–473.

Sengstock, M.C. and Barrett, S. (Spring 1986) 'Elderly victims of family abuse, neglect and maltreatment: Can legal assistance help?, *Journal of Gerontological Social Work, 9,* (3), 43–61.

Social Services Inspectorate (1985) *Inspection of residential care for elderly people and children in the London Borough of Southwark.* London: HMSO.

Social Services Inspectorate (1992) *Confronting elder abuse.* London: HMSO.

Social Services Inspectorate (1993) *Inspecting for quality: standards for the residential care of elderly people with mental disorders*. London: HMSO.

Social Services Inspectorate (1993) *No longer afraid: the safeguard of older people in domestic settings*. London: HMSO.

Solihull Joint Consultative Committee (1994) *Guidelines for managing suspected abuse of vulnerable adults*. Solihull: Solihull Healthcare, Solihull Family Health Services Authority, Solihull MBC Social Services Department, Solihull Health Authority.

Tomlin, S. (1989) *Abuse of elderly people: An unnecessary and preventable problem*. London: British Geriatrics Society.

Wolf, R.S. (1988) 'Elder abuse: Ten years later', *Journal of the American Geriatrics Society*, 36, (8), 758–762.

Appendix 1

Kent County Council Social Services Department Practice Guidelines for Dealing with Elder Abuse

1. Context

1.1 In 1981, the Select Committee on Aging of the United States House of Representative published a report entitled: 'Elder Abuse: An Examination of a Hidden Problem'. In that report, the result of two years of investigation, the Committee concluded:

> '...elder abuse is far from an isolated and localised problem involving a few frail elderly and their pathological offspring. The problem is a full-scale national epidemic which exists with a frequency that few have dared to imagine. In fact, abuse of the elderly by their loved ones and caretakers exists with a frequency only slightly less than child abuse in the United States.'

They concluded that between 5% and 10% of the elderly population was at risk of, or actually suffering, abuse.

1.2 Additional research since 1981 in the United States, and similar research in this country, confirms these early findings, and has added considerably to the body of knowledge now existing on the phenomenon of elderly abuse. 40 of the United States now have systems for mandatory reporting and investigation of adult abuse (of which elder abuse constitutes 82%), unlike this country where there are as yet no systems for mandatory reporting, no legal powers of intervention designed specifically to deal with this problem, and where public and professional awareness of elder abuse is low.

1.3 As long as the legal position in this country remains undefined, the resource implications for the Department remain far less than those for child protection. However, Age Concern (on behalf of the voluntary sector), the British Geriatrics Society (on behalf of the medical professions) and Officers from the London Boroughs of Enfield and Bexley are actively campaigning for the law to be strengthened to give Social Services Departments powers to intervene through the courts when dependent adults are considered to be living in situations of risk. It is therefore simply a matter of time before Kent Social Services Department is faced with dealing with a substantial new set of tasks for elderly consumers in the County, and it is important that both systems and practice are developed while the number of reported cases remains within manageable proportions.

2. Demography

2.1 Never before in this country have so many middle-aged and young-old (65–75) adult children had surviving parents or found themselves having to take care of their ageing parents in the old-old range (75 and over). There are more elderly people than ever before, they are living longer, and their disabilities and dependencies increase in severity with age. With improved nutrition and medical care the expectation of life for adults in this country has increased this century by 25 years. In consequence, the fastest growing sectors of population are the over 25 years. In consequence, the fastest growing sectors of population are the over 85s, followed closely by the over 75s, and the end of this century a third of the population will be over retirement age. It is estimated that the incidence of dementia is 22% or the 80+ population, and some figures place it as high as 30%.

2.2 According to the Office of Population and Censuses, there were in 1987 approximately 6 million carers in this country, of whom 3.5 million are women and 2.5 million men. The potential for worsening family conflict is clear, as the number of dependent elderly people in the population increases and the resources of carers decrease.

2.3 The estimated population of elderly people in Kent in 1991 is 247,500. This means that between 12,000 and 25,000 elderly people in Kent are either at risk of, or currently suffering, abuse.

3. Existing Practice Guidelines

3.1 Practice Guidelines were issued by Kent in 1987 as a result of concerns expressed by fieldwork and residential staff alike (one of the first Social Services Departments to take this action). Though the Department adopted no central system for recording reported time, and reported incidents appear to be increasing with heightened public and professional awareness. Other Departments have now taken or are taking similar action. The listing Guidelines have now been overtaken by the publication of more detailed research and reports improvements in practice systems.

3.2 It is therefore timely that Kent should enhance the Guidelines to take account of these developments. The new Practice Guidelines set out in this document should be adopted operationally as from 1.7.89.

3.3 If Areas feel it would be helpful to mount seminars locally to enhance staff awareness of this issue, input can be provided by staff from Care in the Community Section at Springfield.

Elder Abuse: Practice Guidelines

Definitions

1. Physical abuse, resulting from acts of omission of commission on the part of others, and meaning that the victim's body or bodily functions suffer from some level of pain stemming from the following:

   a. Medical health maltreatment - the consequence of not receiving or being refused medication, receiving too much or too little medication, or receiving medication improperly. Health care may be unavailable when needed or available to an excessive degree, or irregular, improper, inadequate or duplicated in some way.

   b. Bodily impairment - manifested in malnutrition, dehydration, emaciation, poor hygiene, drug or alcohol addiction, sleep deprivation, failure to thrive, unexplained fatigue, hypo/hyperthermia, or improper ventilation.

   c. Bodily assaults - resulting in injuries such as burns, bruises, abrasions, fractures, dislocations, welts, wounds, rashes, pressure sores, or marks of physical restraint.

2. Psychological abuse, resulting from acts of omission or commission on the part of others and producing mental anguish in the victim from the following -

   a. Humiliation - making the older person feel ashamed of his/her involuntary behaviour, blaming the older person for attitudes, actions or events beyond their control, or ridiculing the older person for his/her conduct.

   b. Harassment - episodes of bullying involving being called names, being intimidated, being threatened, being made to fear for life, health or wellbeing, or being shouted at in episodes of rage.

3. Sociological abuse, involving deprivation of normal social contact through acts of omission or commission on the part of others, involving involuntary withdrawal

from valued activity, or inadequate/improper supervision of a person legally defined as requiring care.

4. Legal abuse, resulting from acts of omission or commission on the part of others, involving -
   a. Material exploitation - misuse of the older person's money, property, possessions or insurance, or blocking access to these material goods.
   b. Personal exploitation - denying the rights of a competent elder, or forcing an elder to perform tasks or acts that are inappropriate or inhumane (including sexual abuse).
   c. Theft - through stealing the elder's money, property, possessions or insurance, or extortion of such through threats.

Use of Definitions

1. Abuse of an elder may involve episodes occurring in one, two, three or all four of the above categories.
2. The degree of risk to the elder should be determined by listing actual episodes in each category, and assessing their frequency and intensity. If episodes are increasing in frequency and severity, and/or are occurring in more than one of the above categories, the situation should be considered potentially high risk.

Assessment Guide

1. Factors making abuse more likely to occur:

Research both in the United States and in this country has shown that abuse is more likely to occur if the following factors are present:

1.1 If carers -
   a. feel very lonely and isolated;
   b. habitually lose their temper;
   c. have felt they cannot cope or continue to care for the dependent elder;
   d. perceive the dependent elder as being deliberately awkward;
   e. have to cope with between 2 and 6 major behavioural and/or sexual problems in the dependent elder;
   f. have previously admitted or been seen to shake the dependent elder;
   g. have diminished communication with the dependent elder, either through choice or through incapacity.

1.2 If the dependent elder -
   a. has hit out at the carer;
   b. cannot converse normally;
   c. disturbs the carer at night;
   d. lacks purposeful activity between meals;
   e. exhibits odd or embarrassing behaviours;
   f. is not helpful or co-operative;
   g. is rejecting and/or ungrateful;
   h. has between 5 and 8 negative personality traits.

1.3 The likelihood of abuse occurring is further increased if -
   the carer has other dependants;
   the carer is physically or mentally ill, dependent on drugs or is an alcoholic;
   violence is the norm in the household or establishment;
   fluctuating symptoms of disease are poorly understood;
   the abuser is dependent on the carer for money or accommodation;
   the abuser is young or lacking maturity, and/or feels that the dependent elder failed to fulfil his/her needs for care in former years.

the elder is excluded from outside social contacts.

2. Suspicious signs and symptoms:

a. if the dependent elder is brought to a hospital in emergency by someone other than the caregiver, or is found alone at home in a situation of serious but avoidable risk;

b. if there is a prolonged interval between injury/illness and presentation for medical care, injuries are found at different stages of healing, or such that it is difficult to suggest an accidental cause (e.g. fingermark bruising, cigarette burns, rope-marks on wrists, ankles or neck, or bruising to the inside of upper arms or inside of upper legs);

c. if the dependent elder or caregiver/suspected abuser is known to the police or welfare agencies in circumstances indicating possible risk to the life, health or wellbeing of the elder;

d. if examination of medication indicates that such medication is not being administered as prescribed;

f. if checks with other agencies reveal concerns and/or reports of steadily deteriorating care (e.g. unkempt hair, lost glasses and teeth, lack of care of incontinence, or incidents where elder abuse was suspected.

3. Procedure

3.1 Initial Referral:

A. Every reported incident of elder abuse must be treated with the same urgency as that accorded to incidents of child abuse.

B. The following information should be obtained on receipt of a referral of suspected elder abuse:

  a. Elder's name, address, telephone number, age, gender, and ethnic background (with language spoken if not from the indigenous population).

  b. Elder's close relatives and friends and their telephone numbers, relevant contacts from other agencies involved and their telephone numbers.

  c. Alleged abuser's name, address and telephone number, physical description, and knowledge of his/her behaviour, relationship to elder, and length of relationship.

  d. Description of alleged abuse/neglect, suspicions, and evidence obtained to date. (Dates of prior contacts, action taken and by whom are very helpful.)

  e. GP's name and telephone number, and names and contact numbers for other relevant professionals involved.

  f. Referrer's name and contact telephone number, description of referrer's involvement in case to date, and how long referrer has known elder. (Referrers may in some circumstances wish to remain anonymous, but referrals will nonetheless be investigated.) All referrers giving their name should be warned at the time of referral that their evidence may be needed if they have reported a crime.

C. If the referral is received from another agency, the anticipated involvement of the other agency should be clarified so that roles do not become confused.

D. Every reported incident of domestic abuse must be discussed immediately with a Team Manager or Officer-in-Charge, and investigated by an experienced Home Care Manager.

E. Cases of suspected abuse occurring in private residential care homes should be notified to the appropriate Registration Officer, in addition to action being taken under the procedures described above.

F. Any case of suspected abuse occurring in a K.C.C. establishment must be reported immediately to the local Area Manager within 48 hours, and appropriate action taken immediately.

3.2 Investigation

The investigating Home Care Manager should:

a. Check with other agencies as to whether the dependent elder or alleged abuser is known, and under what circumstances;

b. Check the Department's own records, including the Child Protection Register;

c. Visit accompanied by another worker if circumstances indicate that such precautions are appropriate;

d. Interview the dependent elder alone, without the caregiver, in circumstances in which the elder is certain of privacy;

e. Explain to the caregiver that he/she will be interviewed separately after elder has been interviewed, and that this is normal departmental practice;

f. Work assessment questions into conversation in a relaxed manner and not rush the elder or the caregiver while being interviewed. (If interpreting services are required, care must be taken to ensure that the interpreter is someone independent of the elder's family, and recognised as competent to fulfil this role.);

g. Take care not to diagnose an elder prematurely as being abused or neglected, and not suggest possible treatments plans until all the facts are known;

h. Pay special attention to suspicious signs and symptoms and the known precipitating factors for abuse as listed in these Guidelines;

i. Make a preliminary assessment of the mental capacity of the dependent elder.

3.3 Subsequent Action

A. The police should be informed if it is suspected that there is prima facie evidence that a crime has been committed against person or property.

B. Referral should be made to a GP so that an appropriate medical examination of the dependent elder can be made immediately, with the informed consent of the elder if possible. If injuries are found, they should be mapped on a body chart.

C. Arrangements to protect an elder at risk must be made as soon as possible. A case conference involving all professionals concerned (and wherever possible the elder and caregiver) should be arranged within 72 hours and held within 10 days. At this conference, information will be fully shared, action planned, and careful records made of the investigation and subsequent action taken.

D. If there is urgent need to protect an abused elder, such an elder will have priority to obtain a bed in a residential unit, provided he/she is willing to go. If medical care, or an opinion as to the elder/s competence to make such a decision, is required, negotiations should be urgently undertaken through the elder's GP to obtain this.

3.4 Registration

If, at a multidisciplinary case conference, either -

a. the abuse is proved, or

b. the abuse is very strongly suspected, but actual proof has not been obtained, or

c. the abuse is proved, but the elder elects to remain in a situation of potential continuation of such abuse -

A. The case must be kept open, and allocated to a suitably experienced Home Care Manager.

B. Efforts should be made to involve the elder in outside activities as appropriate, to reduce risks and facilitate monitoring.

C. Respite care/phased care should be encouraged, to reduce family conflict and facilitate monitoring.

D. Attempts should be made to put the elder in contact with a suitable advocate who can represent his/her interests.

E. If financial abuse is suspected, advice may be sought as appropriate from the elder's solicitor, Bank Manager, Building Society Manager, or D.S.S. Officer, who may undertake home visits to advise the elder. Application may be made to the Court of Protection in appropriate cases.

F. The case should be formally reviewed every six months, while the elder remains in the situation in which the abuse/suspected abuse occurred. The Chairperson of the review should not hold line management responsibility for day-to-day case management.

3.5 Records

Areas will keep local records of cases of elder abuse registered, using the definitions outlined in these Guidelines. Such registers are intended to enable the Department to check the numbers of such cases currently being reported, and any trends that may be emerging. A record should be kept at the Area Office of each such case, with the name, address, I.D. number (M.I.S.), age, date of birth, and the category/categories of abuse recorded, together with the date of the initial referral and initial case conference.

3.6 Staff Support

Kent Social Services Department recognises that, with only limited legal powers (the Mental Health Act, 1983, and Section 47 of the National Assistance Act, 1948, which will only apply in rare cases), elders at risk may sometimes remain in dangerous situations because staff have no power to gain access to them, remove them from such a situation, investigate the conduct of their affairs - or because the elder him/herself refuses all help. Staff will be expected to continue to exercise as much vigilance as possible in these circumstances. However, the Department will give full support to staff over problems of handling such high risk cases, provided it is evident from case records that procedures have been followed and that there is no action that could have been taken to provide further safeguards for the elder at risk.

Appendix 2

London Borough of Enfield
Notes of Guidance (Practice and Procedure)
Abuse of Vulnerable Adults (1993)

1. Introduction
1.1 The purpose of these guidelines is to highlight the problem of physical, emotional and financial abuse of vulnerable adults by informal/formal carers.

1.2 The guidelines are based on good practice within existing resources and were drawn together by a small working party comprising of Social Services, Health staff and frontline workers and managers. The police were represented on the working party by the Community and Youth Section of the Metropolitan Police.

1.3 Policy of the Metropolitan Police Service

1.3.1 Metropolitan Police 1 Area (North) Crime Strategy 1991–1995 in partnership with the community and in cooperation with both statutory and voluntary agencies, to provide a quality of service conducive to the creation of an environment within which people may live in safety and enjoy an enhanced quality of life. The achievement of this strategy will be through the development and promotion of practices aimed at reducing the number of victims of criminal and anti-social behaviour.

1.3.2 It is paramount that vulnerable adults should have the full protection of the law, as it is the right of every member of the community.

Whilst it is the duty of Police to investigate allegations of crimes and to initiate court prosecutions against suggested offenders, it is acknowledged that even when there is sufficient evidence that a crime has been committed, a successful prosecution could not be instigated because of the victim's inability to give evidence; i.e., witnesses, because of the victim's fear of the subsequent repercussions to their own life style. Because of these factors and the influences Police appreciate the joint working practice to enable allegations of crime to be resolved by joint case conferencing or counselling when considered the most suitable solution.

1.4 The aims of the working party were:

1.4.1 To define abuse of vulnerable adults in its various aspects

1.4.2 To improve both practice and service delivery to vulnerable adults suffering from abuse.

1.4.3 To gather local information and knowledge on the subject and through these guidelines create a greater awareness amongst all the relevant professionals and agencies.

2. Defining Abuse
2.1 The lack of a precise, comprehensive definition of abuse has, until recently, hindered efforts to determine the extent of the problem and form a basic framework within which all disciplines can work together.

2.2 The working party examined a number of possible definitions and whether Enfield should have one at all. James Callaham (1986) has argued that any single definition is too restricting and would rule out some important abuse-related facets. Others, however, including the working party regard this both as evading the issue and causes difficulties in establishing who is excluded/included within any practice guidelines.

2.3 A working definition is suggested:

2.3.1 'THE PHYSICAL, EMOTIONAL OR PSYCHOLOGICAL ABUSE OF A VULNERABLE ADULT BY A FORMAL OR INFORMAL CARER. THE ABUSE IS REPEATED AND IS THE VIOLATION BY A PERSON/OR PERSONS WHO HAVE POWER OVER THE LIFE OF A DEPENDENT.'

2.4 The definition outlined in paragraph 2.3.1 covers institutional abuse as well as abuse in the home, and includes the key concepts of dependency, power and violation.

2.5 In order, however, to formulate an appropriate Social Services procedure, it is perhaps more helpful to identify the practices which constitute abuse. In broad terms, they follow the general police framework which the working party considered helpful.

2.5.1 **Simple Assault**: pushing, thumping, forced medication, pulling hair, etc.

2.5.2 **Actual Bodily Harm**: physical sign of assault from reddening to actual fracture. Within this category emotional abuse is included, whereby the action/inaction of a carer has a clear emotional/psychological impact on the vulnerable adult.

2.5.3 **Grievous Bodily Harm**: unlawful wounding, including cuts, or use of a weapon that causes actual injury.

2.5.4 **Grievous Bodily Harm with Intent**: any intended action/act of causing injury.

2.5.5 **Manslaughter.**

2.5.6 **Murder.**

2.5.7 **Theft**: a person is guilty of theft if she/he dishonestly appropriates property, belonging to another, with intention of permanently depriving the owner of it.

2.5.8 Financial Crime:

This has many facets, from the crimes of forging signatures on pension books and encashing them, to the manipulation of the victim's intentions when drawing up wills. Primarily one must have a victim and criminal intent by the suspect. With complicated cases there is a grey area between criminal law and civil law.

i.e., disputes by beneficiaries and the probate of wills. If there is any doubt inform your line manager who will refer for advice to the Legal Section within the Corporate Services Department or to the Police as 7.3.

2.6 In more social work/health terminology abuse is also seen within the following context, but can be cross referenced to sections 2.5.1 to 2.5.6 above.

2.6.1 Physical assault, including pushing, punching, pinching, slapping, forced feeding, forced medication and restrictions on movement, hot and cold baths.

2.6.2 Threats of physical assault/actions.

2.6.3 Neglect, including refusing to supply meals, rejecting various types of appropriate support and totally ignoring the vulnerable person's presence, e.g. 24 hour wearing of nightwear.

2.6.4 Sexual abuse and interference (threatened or actual).

2.6.5 Abandonment to residential care or hospital care, including the threat 'to put away' and the threat to withdraw from caring.

2.6.6 Exploitation, including the appropriation of money and property.

2.6.7 Psychological abuse, including shouting, screaming, intimidation and a whole range of threats.

2.6.8 Denial of basic human rights, including choice, opinion and privacy.

3. Known Reactions to Abuse

3.1 The identification of cases of abuse, even where there may be signs of physical damage is unlikely to be simple and will usually require the collation of often small pieces of information from a variety of sources.

3.2 The current research available suggests the more common reactions are indications of abuse, not necessarily evidence, as follows:

    3.2.1 The denial (often forthright) that anything is amiss, with an accompanying emphasis that things 'could hardly be better'.

    3.2.2 Resignation, stoicism, and, sometimes, an acceptance of incidents as being part of being old/vulnerable.

    3.2.3 Withdrawal from activity, communication and participation.

    3.2.4 Marked change of behaviour and inappropriate attachments. Fear, frequently combined with depression and a sense of hopelessness.

    3.2.5 Mental confusion.

    3.2.6 Anger and physical/verbal outbursts.

    3.2.7 Seeking (attention/protection), often from numerous sources (some of which can be unlikely).

4. Physical Indication of Abuse

4.1 The following injuries should arouse suspicion, and therefore should be the subject of thorough investigation (see Guidelines Section 7 below).

    4.1.1 Multiple bruising, not consistent with a fall.

    4.1.2 Black eyes, slap marks, kick marks, other bruises.

    4.1.3 Burns, not consistent with scorching by direct heat.

    4.1.4 Fractures not consistent with falls.

    4.1.5 Stench of urine or faeces.

    4.1.6 Indications of malnutrition or over-feeding.

    4.1.7 Absence of mobility aids.

    4.1.8 Administration of inappropriate drugs, or the absence of necessary medication.

5. Institutional Abuse

5.1 The standard of care in both public and private residential homes has in recent years received a great deal of publicity. Whilst a sub-standard of care certainly does prevail, there are also many in which vulnerable adults are cared for with compassion and sensitivity.

5.2 With regard to the abuse of vulnerable adults in institutions, consideration must be given to the fact that there are two different understandings of the phrase 'institutional abuse' (Tomlin 1989).

    5.2.1 There is individual abuse, where a resident or residents are hit, are verbally abused or have their money stolen or misused.

        a. Residents awakened too early in the morning.

        b. Lack of flexibility in choice in the time of going to bed.

        c. Lack of opportunity for getting drinks and snacks.

        d. Lack of choice and consultation about meals, the last meal being served too early.

        e. Lack of personal possessions, furniture, telephone, T.V. radio, etc.

        f. Lack of procedure for washing, mending and marking personal clothing.

        g. Lack of toileting facilities.

        h. Clothing dirty and unkempt, often with no underwear.

        i. Inappropriate handling of medical complaints.

j. Lack of opportunity for social contact outside the home.

5.3 Guidance has been produced with regard to practices in residential care. It is important to note that this section is intended to highlight those factors that can constitute, in current research terms, institutional abuse and should therefore not be taken as implicitly inferring abuse taken place within Enfield's residential provision.

5.4 Possible Signs of Institutional Abuse

    5.4.1 Individual abuse (see sections 2.5.2 to 2.6.8, exclude 2.6.5 abandonment).

    5.4.2 Institutional abuse (that can lead to individual abuse).

        a. Failure to agree within the managing agency about the purpose or/and tasks of the home.

        b. Failure to manage life in the centre/home in an appropriate way. (When things go wrong they are not sorted out e.g. maintenance of building.)

        c. Poor standards of cleanliness.

        d. Low staffing levels over a long period of time.

        e. Lack of knowledge or confusion about guidelines.

        f. Breakdown of communication between managers of the home.

        g. Staff factions (result often of f.).

        h. Staff working the hours to suit them.

        i. Staff may drink heavily on or off duty.

        j. Staff ordering residents around or even shouting at them.

        k. Lack of positive communication with residents.

        l. Low staff morale.

        m. Failure by management to see a pattern of events which are often treated as individual instances in isolation.

        n. Punitive methods adopted by staff against residents.

5A. Powers under Registered Homes Act

5A.1 The Registered Homes Act 1984 and its regulations and Amendments give the Local authority the duty to register all homes and inspect residential homes of four or more beds which provide board and personal care for elderly people, people recovering from mental illness, people with learning disabilities, people recovering from drug or alcohol abuse and people with physical disabilities.

5A.2 From April 1993 homes with three or fewer beds will also be Registered but not inspected unless there is a complaint.

5A.3 Registered Officers have powers of entry to any premises they reasonably believe to be residential home. to obstruct this would be a criminal offence subject to heavy fine.

5A.4 A home which operated unregistered can be prosecuted at Magistrates Court. It is a criminal offence and again subject to heavy fine.

5A.5 Homes which are registered can have their Registration cancelled for the following reasons:

    5A.5.1 Any which lead to refusal, i.e.

        (a) proprietor and/or Manager are 'unfit' to carry on a home.

        (b) the premises, staffing, equipment etc., provided by the homes are unsuitable.

        (c) The way in which the home is being run is not so as to provide facilities or services reasonably required.

    5A.5.2 The annual fee in respect of the home has not been paid.

5A.5.3 That an offence has been committed by the person registered in respect of the home under the Act or the Regulations; or that the conditions on the Registration Certificate have not been complied with.

5A.6 The person whose Registration is refused or cancelled has right of appeal and the home remains operational whilst this procedure is followed. There is a large amount of case law governing the Act and tribunals take account of this.

5A.7 If it is believed that the residents health, welfare or well being is at serious risk the Registration Officers can apply to Magistrates for an urgent cancellation of Registration when the home is de-registered forthwith, pending any appeal process.

6. Case Management—The Vulnerable Adult at Home

6.1 The case management framework is proposed to cover any domestic setting and is inclusive of a domestic home, family base and private/voluntary homes of three or less individuals who pay for their care but excluded from the Registered Homes Act (1983) and group homes.

    6.1.1 The use of legislation.

    6.1.2 The collation of relevant information.

    6.1.3 Liaison with police.

    6.1.4 The use of the case conference.

    6.1.5 The type of intervention used.

6.2 Under existing powers, the local authority (and in some circumstances the health authority) have both duties and discretions, to take certain steps to ensure that vulnerable people are protected and their interests represented. This is done through the number of Acts of Parliament and set out below are a few of the more important and more well known provisions:

    6.2.1 **National Assistance Act 1948**

    Section 47 of the Act enables a local authority to make an application to a Magistrates Court to remove a person from his home on the grounds:

        a. That the person is suffering from grave chronic disease or being aged or infirm or physically incapacitated, is living in insanitary conditions;

        b. That the person is unable to devote to himself and is not receiving from other persons proper care and attention;

        c. That his removal from home is necessary either in his own interests or for preventing injury to the health of, or serious nuisance to other persons.

    6.2.2 **Mental Health Act 1983**

        a. Part II of the Act deals with the compulsory admission of persons suffering from mental illness to hospitals and guardianship:

            i. Section 2 authorises compulsory admission to hospital for assessment and for detention for this purpose for up to 28 days.

            ii. Section 3 allows a similar detention but for treatment, for up to six months.

            iii. Section 7 deals with guardianship and specifies the circumstances whereby a person aged 16 or over may be received into the guardianship of a local Social Services authority or person who is acceptable to the authority , or Section 8 can confer powers over the person so received, to allow management office affairs.

        b. Part VII of the Act (Section 93–3113) is concerned with the powers of the Court of Protection over the management of the property and affairs of persons incapable, by reason of mental disorder, of managing their own affairs. Application to the Court of Protection is usually made by the person's nearest relative or some other person including a doctor, or social worker can apply.

   c. Section 115 provides approved social workers with a power to enter and inspect a premises where a mentally disordered patient is believed to be living. The power does not apply to hospitals; does not allow forced entry (although in a sense obstruction makes this); and can only be exercised within the area of the approved social worker's employing authority.

6.2.3 Disabled Persons (Services Consultation and Representation) Act 1986

   a.The aim of this statute is to impose the rights of disabled persons by enabling them to have greater say in the provision of services and by clarifying the obligations of local authorities to assess the needs of disabled persons.

      i. Section 1 enables regulations to be made to provide for the appointments of representatives by disabled persons on their behalf. The rights of the authorised representatives and the obligations on the local authority to provide them with the opportunities to represent the disabled persons are set out in Sections 2 and 3.

      ii. Other obligations upon the local authority are constraint throughout the Act.

6.3 Professional Issues with Regard to Situations that Appear to Fall into Outside Existing Legislation

   6.3.1 From time to time a situation may be prevented where an individual client is vulnerable from neglect (self or carer) where access is denied or refused.

6.4 The Enfield Perspective

   6.4.1 Section 135 of the Mental Health Act would make access possible should it deemed necessary.

   6.4.2 The Common Law Principal of Necessity should not be used.

   6.4.3 Unless the criteria of the Section 47 is satisfied it is unlikely that the access would be permissible under the National Assistance Act 1948.

6.5 Conclusions

   6.5.1 Access is possible and existing legislation would enable social service staff to gain access into an individual's home, where the primary carer or client refuses.

   6.5.2 In terms of assessment the principal of good practice would, it is hoped, establish a multidisciplinary approach. One would also refer to Abuse of Vulnerable Adult Guidelines (1) in these circumstances.

   6.5.3 The key components of good intervention at this stage depend on:

      (a)Clear understanding on the roles of each member of a multidisciplinary team.

      (b)The appointment of a key worker.

      (c)Clear communication.

      (d)Prioritising.

6.6 Intervention

Intervention is best illustrated by the attached flow chart that maps out the option open if avenues are closed e.g. referral (Appendix One).

N.B. During 1990 guidelines will be produced on 'consent to Treatment' which are currently under consultation. These will be extremely detailed and may supersede these present guidance notes.

6.7 It is the intention of the Social Services Department that where an emergency admission is deemed necessary for the protection of a vulnerable adult this should be facilitated within existing resources. In the event that immediate protection is not available, reference should be made to the Assistant Director of Social Services or the Deputy Director.

NO PERSON SHOULD BE LEFT IN A VULNERABLE ENVIRONMENT AND AT RISK OF ABUSE.

7. Guidelines

7.1 On suspicion of abuse, worker records the reason for suspicion using the aforementioned sections.

7.2 Consult with line manager to determine:

    7.2.1 Verification of 7.1

    7.2.2 Determine category of abuse.

7.3 If category of abuse falls within the definition of sections 2.5.1 to 2.5.8 contact the Deputy Community Liaison Officer for Enfield Borough at _____ or to Police as 7.3.

    7.3.1 If category of abuse falls within 2.5.3 and 2.5.4, referral to the policy should not be delayed by invoking the procedure at 7.3, and the referral should be made direct to the local policy station for the area covered because of the nature of the offence.

7.4 The Legal Section within the Corporate Services Department are available to Social Services for *ad hoc* and urgent advice in any case where abuse of a vulnerable adult is suspected.

7.5 Staff who suspect abuse may have occurred should express their concern but not hold any investigation at this stage; they should immediately make contact with the police as outlined in 7.3 and 7.3.1 above.

7.6 Depending on the seriousness of the abuse the following information should be determined and a case conference arranged.

    7.6.1 Essential information will include:

        a. The mental and physical health of both the vulnerable adult and the carer.

        b. Family composition and relationship.

        c. Financial information (including the responsibility for the finances of the vulnerable adult).

        d. The domestic setting, general condition, sleeping arrangement.

        e. The content of the social network of both the vulnerable adult and the carer.

        f. The level and the nature of support provided and accepted or refused, plus the support requested by not offered.

    7.6.2 It may be that the information provided does not warrant a case conference and this decision rests with the Service Manager in consultation with the appropriate Professional Adviser.

7.7 In the event that a conference is decided it should include people who can contribute to an understanding of the case and who should therefore be party to the recommendations e.g. social services, Housing (Special Needs), police, D.S.S. Officer, health personnel, medical staff (general practitioners, doctors).

7.8 Careful consideration should be given to inviting the vulnerable adult and/or the informal carer, unless there are specific reasons why not.

8. Appropriate Working Methods

8.1 There are two components to these which should be recognised at the case conference which will recommend the level and type of intervention to be followed in respect of both the vulnerable adult and carer.

1. The direct work with the individual family.

2. The co-ordinated response of all involved.

8.2 Any method of working where abuse has occurred should be directed at both the abused and the abuser(s).

8.3 The method chosen should depend upon an assessment of the cause of abuse. There is little evidence to confirm the effectiveness of any particular form of action, but what evidence there is suggests that it is important not to see abuse as a symptom of a total breakdown in the particular caring network involved, but as a result of stresses and other difficulties that require attention.

8.4 Any work methods that are chosen by the case conference need to concern themselves primarily with the following objectives:

8.4.1 Removing or modifying where possible the factors that make abuse more likely.

8.4.2 Assisting the abused and abuser to re-establish their relationships.

8.4.3 Assisting the abused and the abuser to overcome the fear, guilt or other emotional responses that will make it difficult for them to function normally in the future.

8.4.4 Where an analysis of the risk factors demonstrate that abuse is very likely to happen again the opportunity to remove from the situation should be offered to the abused.

8.4.5 That where abuse is of a nature determined by the police to warrant proceedings, attempt should be paid to supporting the abused and abuser.

8.5 Co-ordination

8.5.1 It is essential that the response of those involved is co-ordinated and based on the principle/objective outlined in sections 8.4.1 to 8.4.5.

8.5.2 This requires that:

a. Shared guidelines are understood by all agencies.

b. An effective and efficient communication network is operated.

c. That all the agencies involved are committed to the objective and their guidelines.

8.6 Whatever form of intervention is adopted initially, it must be subject to regular evaluation in order to assess the effectiveness over time. Additional conferences should be convened when modification to the service responses would appear to be necessary, in addition to the review process.

9. Carer's Notes of Guidance

9.1 The intention of cross referral to the Carer's Guidelines is to ensure that the investigation of abuse takes into account the principles and values of supporting informal carers.

9.1.1 Normally there are two victims of abuse, the carer and the vulnerable adult.

9.1.2 see Appendix A for copy of the guidelines.

10. Management Response – The Vulnerable Adult as Service User in Residential Care/Day Care/Home Care

10.1 It is the duty of all staff working in residential care or visiting to report to their line manager any witnesses incident(s) of abuse. The Registered Homes Act 1983 is also designed to protect vulnerable adults and reference should be made to the Department's Registered Homes Section where the home falls within the private/voluntary sector.

10.1.1 Should the abuse be suspected or witnessed within a private nursing home please follow the same guidelines as 10.1.

10.2 The management systems employed to support and supervise staff in their work and to facilitate good communications are vital if the potential for abuse is to be reduced to its lowest possible level. Managers must ensure that all staff are aware of these guidance notes and staff are expected to take responsibility for being familiar with its content.

10.3 There must be staff team strategies to raise the awareness of staff and to provide them with the personal and professional skills which enable them to cope.

10.4 Managers are expected to ensure all staff within their unit/establishment are clear about direct and indirect care tasks and the dignity of users is maintained at all times.

10.5 The way in which the home relates to the outside world can be of critical importance and the departmental aim and process should be clearly understood by all staff (refer also 5.2.1 (j)).

10.6 Response Guidelines to Suspected Abuse

> 10.6.1 The care case management framework used for people living in their own home is recommended and should commence with:
>> a. Report to Directorate and Inspection Unit of suspected or witnessed abuse.
>> b. Inspection Unit to determine category of abuse.
>
> 10.6.2 If category of abuse falls within the definition of section 2.5.2 to 2.5.8 the Directorates and Inspection Unit will refer to the appropriate Professional Adviser. Independent/Private Inspection will inform Professional Adviser who will decide if they need to be involved. The Directorate and/or Inspection Unit will determine the involvement of police.
>
> 10.6.3 Consideration will be made to determine whether the alleged abuser is identified and steps taken to deal with the member of staff in consultation with central personnel/Social Service personnel.
>
> 10.6.4 It is clear that not every single incident/allegation would be referred to the policy (see 10.6.2) but if referral is made no interview or investigation should commence. Please liaise closely with the Directorate and/or appropriate Professional Adviser.
>
> 10.6.5 If theft is suspected then the police should in any event be notified by the reporting officer.
>
> 10.6.6 In the event of suspension of the member of staff the Council's Procedure on Disciplinary Action should be followed.
>
> 10.6.7 The resident abused should be offered appropriate counselling. Manager/inspector is responsible for monitoring that this is accomplished (i.e. Home Care, Service Manager, Area Manager etc.).
>
> 10.6.10 In the event that abuse is alleged by a visitor of family member, this matter should be dealt with in accordance with the department's COMPLAINTS PROCEDURE.
>
> 10.6.11 If a case conference model is decided the procedure outlined in Section 8 should be adopted.

11. Restraint (Slater 1988)

11.1 During the course of the working party it was recognised that sometimes there is a need for those who care for vulnerable people to exercise some degree of management and control.

11.2 Legal and other professional texts have seldom given guidance as to the rights and responsibilities of staff exercising force over vulnerable adults. The questions are not only academic but have profound practical importance.

11.2.1 The use of such force to restrain can in certain cases, without a lawful justification, constitute a trespass to the person. This is not only a civic wrong but is also a criminal offence.

11.2.2 Preservation of Life – plainly, restraint that is immediately necessary to preserve life can be used where the person is non-volitional.

11.2.3 Prevention of Harm – it is suggested that the doctrine of necessity would probably provide sufficient protection for the staff member who used reasonable force which was immediately necessary to prevent an incompetent patient (mental health) vulnerable adult from coming to any obvious and significant harm.

11.2.4 Within the context of 11.2.3 above, wandering residents would be included, in that staff must act reasonably in attempting to discourage a resident from wandering where in all reasonable judgement the resident faces unacceptable risk (e.g. road accident, etc).

Additional sources
Callaham, J. Pride Institute of Longterm Home Care 1986;5:3.
Tomlin, S. Abuse of Elderly People - A Public Information Guide from B.G.S. (1989).
Slater, P. Mental Health - A Social Services Staff Development Manual II:4.

Incident/Concern recording form *
Abuse of vulnerable adults
*NB This form covers all types of abuse i.e. specific incident or concerns/suspicions about ongoing abuse.

Service User Name:

Residence address at time of incident/concern:

Where or how did the incident/concern occur:
(if applicable)

Time: Date:

Who was involved (please specify if staff were involved i.e. post held, relationship of abuser to person abused etc.).
Name(s):

Name of manager to whom this incident/concern was reported:

Nature of incident/concern: (please give details as fully as possible, including an opinion if possible of perceived degree of severity i.e. major, minor etc.)

Action taken:

By whom:

(NB A referral of any incident/concern should automatically be made to the relevant Professional Adviser (by the quickest method i.e. telephone/fax etc.), in addition to involvement by line managers)

Referred to Professional Adviser .... Name............. Date
.... Person recording incident/concern ....
(signature)   (date)

Completed form to be returned as promptly as possible to: Information Section, Social Services
Copy to be retained by the Area/Unit.

Comments on incident/concern to be completed by Professional Adviser
Name.. Date..................

Completed section to be returned as promptly as possible to: Information Section

For Information Section Use Only:
Copy forwarded to Inspectorate □   Date.........................

Action By Inspectorate

Officer Dealing ....   Date..............
Copy to be returned to Information Section, Social Services.
A final copy of all completed sections will be returned to the Area/Unit for reference.

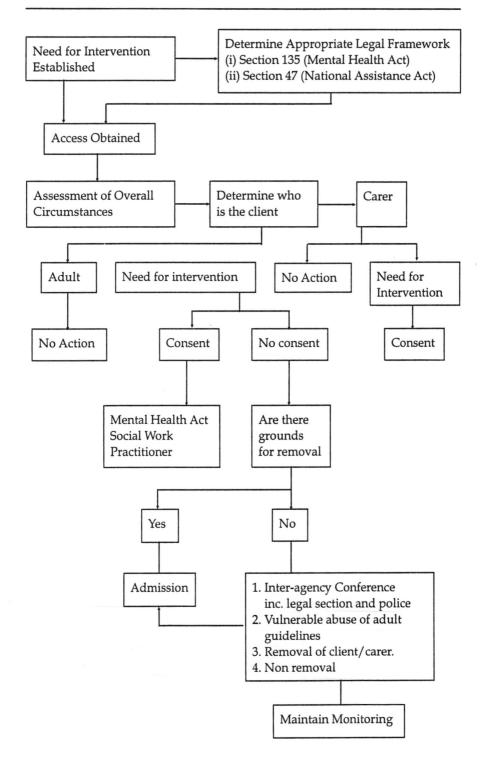

Appendix 3

A Bodychart

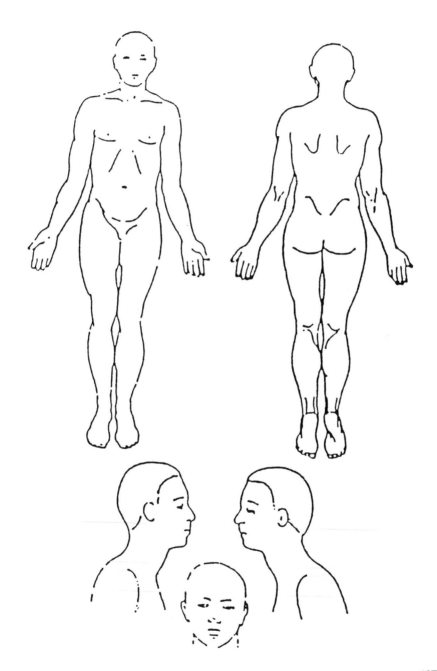

Index

abandonment to care 24, 185
abuse definitions *see* definitions
'abuse' exercise 92
abuse history as causal factor 30, 36
abuse types 19–22, 23–5, 26, 76
abusers 24, 51
  characteristics 73–5, 73, 74, 75
  resources to help 64–5, 79, 79–80
  social history 37–9
  training exercise 101
access to mentally incapacitated people 62
active abuse 26
Adults at Risk 24
ADSS (Association of the Directors of Social Services) 24
advocates 67

age
  of abusers 73, 73, 74
  of victims 71, 72
Age Concern 98, 111
ageism 16
alcoholism 31
arrears, as sign of abuse 45
assessment 37–9, 54, 55, 67–8
asset protection 63–4
asset selling, as sign of abuse 47
Association of the Directors of Social Services (ADSS) 24
'at risk' registers 58–9
  training exercises 101, 115
Attorney, Power of 64
awareness raising 17, 49–50, 68–9

Barrett, S. 101, 111
BASW 96

Bedford Social Services Department 106
behaviour change 44–5
body charts 100, 196
Bookin, D. 103

Callahan, J. 23
carers 21–2, 24, 36
  institutional staff as 34–5
  as victims 29
  see also stress
case conferences 56–8, 59–60
  training exercises 116, 136–51
casualty department visits 59
causal factors 35–6
  training exercise 103
child abuse links 30–1
Community Care Survey 70

confidentiality 53
Confronting Elder Abuse 24
confusion, as abuse sign 45
co-ordination of services *see* multidisciplinary approach
Cornell, C.P. 73
Court of Protection 63–4
Crossroads Care 108

Davies, M. 100
day care 65, 66
debts, as sign of abuse 45
Decalmer, P. 100
definitions of abuse 15–27
  guidelines 22–6, 179–80, 184–5
  training exercises 91–8
deliberate abuse 31–2
denial of abuse 44, 50, 51
denial of basic human rights 24, 185
Department of Social Security 63
dependency factors 35–6
depression 45

'developing skills' exercise 104
difficult behaviour problems 36
disclosing abuse 47, 51, 53, 68
Douglass, R.L. 103
drug abuse 31–2
Dunkle, R.E. 103

Eastman, M. 19–20, 70, 71, 93, 97, 102
'economic factors' exercise 103
elder abuse, as taboo subject 15–16, 17
'elder abuse' exercise 93
emergency beds 66
emotional abuse 20, 21, 25, 76
  carers as victims 29
  Enfield guidelines 24, 185
emotional neglect 41
Enduring Power of Attorney 64
Enfield *see* London Borough of Enfield
environmental problems 36
exercises 91–172
  recognizing abuse 99–108
  scenarios 164–72
  what is abuse 91–8, 117–21

working with abuse 109–16, 122–5
  case conferences 136–51
  role play exercises 126–35
  simulation 152–63
exploitation 24, 185

family placement schemes 66
family relationship problems 36
financial abuse 20, 21, 25, 76
  carers as victims 29
  law 62–4
  signs of 39, 45–7
  training exercise 105
financial problems 36
Finkelhor, D. 101
frequency of abuse 78
frequency of requests for help 50, 59

gang abuse 32–3, 53–4
Garrett, G. 108
gay men, sexual abuse of 43
Gelles, R.J. 73
gender
  of abusers 73
  of victims 71
Gilleard, C. 108
Glendenning, F. 100
Gostin, L. 62, 111

'granny bashing' 70
Griffiths, A. 111
Guardianship Orders
   62
guidelines 22–6,
   59–60, 79
   Kent Social Services
   22–3, 178–83
   London Borough of
   Enfield 23–4, 25,
   184–95
   training exercises
   95–6

health monitoring
   39–40
hearing about abuse
   77–8, 78
helplines 67
Hickey, T. 103
Hildrew, M.A. 22
Hocking, E.D. 70, 100
Holt, M.G. 43
homemakers 66–7
Homer, A.C. 108
honesty 53

ignoring abuse 51
incest 43
indications of abuse
   see signs
injunctions 61
injuries 39, 40, 55
   Sheffield study
   76–7, 76, 77
   training exercise 100

institutional abuse
   34–5, 67
   training exercises
   106–7
institutional
   management
   problems 19
'interviewing skills'
   exercise 114,
   126–35
isolation of carers 37,
   66

Kent Social Services
   Department
   guidelines 22–3,
   96, 178–83
key workers 55, 60

law 60–4
   training exercise
   111–12
Law Commission 61,
   111
legal abuse 23, 180
listening to victims
   50, 68
London Borough of
   Enfield guidelines
   23–4, 25, 184–95
   use in training
   exercises 96, 98,
   107, 111
loyalty 38

marital violence 29–30

medical problems
   of abusers 75
   of victims 71, 72
medication,
   administering 39,
   41
Mental Health Act
   (1983) 62, 64
mentally
   incapacitated
   older people 61–2
'Monday morning
   in-tray' exercise
   113, 122–5
monitoring cases 54,
   55
multidisciplinary
   approach 25–6,
   52–4
   training exercise 97
multiple dependency
   factors 35–6
mutual abuse 30

National Assistance
   Act (1948) and
   Amendment
   (1951) 61
neglect 20, 21, 41–2
   Enfield guidelines
   24, 185
night care 65
No Longer Afraid: the
   safeguard of older
   people in domestic
   settings 24

occupation of abusers 74, 75
offences, chargeable 60–1
Old Age Abuse 70
opposition to elder abuse 15–16, 17
Oxford English Dictionary 15, 41

passive abuse 26
pension books, misuse of 63
permanent care 65
personal gain, abuse for 31–2
personal problems
of abusers 31, 36, 75
of victims 36, 71, 72
personality changes 44–5
physical abuse 19–21, 25, 76
carers as victims 29
Enfield guidelines 24, 185
Kent guidelines 23, 179
signs 39–44, 40, 76–7, 76, 77
physical neglect 41
physical outbursts 45
physical problems
of abusers 75
of victims 71, 72
physical signs of abuse 39–42, 40

Sheffield study 76–7, 76, 77
Pillemer, K. 101
'police perspective' exercise 98
Power of Attorney 64
powers of entry and inspection 62
pre-meditated abuse 31–2
primary workers 60
Pritchard, J. H. 33, 35, 37, 101, 108
procedures see guidelines
professional
dilemmas 19, 27, 51
training exercises 94, 117–21
professionals
different views of abuse 17–18
multidisciplinary approach 25–6, 52–4
raising awareness 68–9
training exercises 97, 98
views on resources 66–7
psychological abuse 25
Enfield guidelines 24, 185
Kent guidelines 23, 179

psychological/psychiatric problems 36
Public Trust Office 64, 111

quality of life 27

reactions to abuse 44–5, 186
example 81–90
training exercise 102
recognition of abuse 28–48
causal factors 35–6
exercises 99–108
likely situations 28–35
signs 39–44, 40, 45–7
social history 37–9
stress and carers 36–7
victims' reactions 44–5
refuges 67
registers, 'at risk' 58–9
training exercise 115
relationship between victims and abusers 74, 74
reminiscence 38
removal of victims from home 61, 64–5
research studies 70
see also Sheffield research study

resources 64–8
  future 66–8
  Sheffield study
    79–80, *79–80*
  training exercise 110
respite care 65, 66
reviewing abuse
  cases 55–6
rights, basic human
  26–7
Riley, P. 19, 94
Roberts, G. 111
role play exercises
  114, 126–35
  case conferences
    136–51
  simulation 152–63
'role reversal' marital
  violence 30
Royal College of
  Nursing 26

Sanford, J.R.A. 108
scenario examples for
  training use
  164–72
self neglect 20
Sengstock, M.C. 101,
  111
sexual abuse 20, 21,
  24, 51
  disclosing 38
  signs 42–3, 45
Sheffield research
  study 70, 71–80
  abusers 73–6, *73, 74,*
    75

frequency of abuse
  78
hearing about
  abuse 77–8, *78*
intervention and
  outcome 79,
  79–80
type of abuse 76–7,
  76, 77
victims 71–3, *72*
short-term care 65, 66
signing over
  property 46
signs of abuse 39–48
  behaviour 44–5
  financial 45–7
  physical 39–44, *40*
  training exercises
    102, 104
simulation exercises
  152–63
sitting services 66
'skills development'
  exercise 104
'social factors'
  exercise 103
social histories of
  victims and
  abusers 37–8
Social Services
  Inspectorate (SSI)
  21, 22, 24, 93, 96
sociological abuse 23,
  25, 179–80
Solihull Joint
  Consultative
  Committee 58–9,
  115

SSI *see* Social Services
  Inspectorate
staffing issues,
  institutions 34–5
stress, carers' 28–9,
  36–7
  institutional staff 35
  relieving 65, 66
  training exercise 108
Swindon study 70

Times 32
trust 51, 53

'unintentional' abuse
  21–2

verbal outbursts 45
victims
  characteristics 71–3,
    72, 74, 74
  'how it feels' 81–8
  resources to help
    64–6, 79, *79–80*
  social history 37–9
  views on help
    needed 67
  'who is at risk'
    exercise 101
voluntary sector 66
'vulnerable adults'
  23, 24, 58–9, 184

'who is at risk?'
  exercise 101

Williams, J. 111
withdrawn
    behaviour 44–5
working with abuse
    49–69
  assessment and
      monitoring 55
  'at risk' registers
      58–9
  case conferences
      56–8
  exercises 109–16
  law 60–4
  multidisciplinary
      approach 52–4
  procedures and
      guidelines 59–60
  resources 64–8
  reviewing 55–6
  simple rules 50–2

Good Practice Series

Edited by Jacki Pritchard

This new series explores topics of current concern to professionals working in social work, health care and the probation service. Contributors are drawn from a wide variety of settings, in both the voluntary and statutory sectors.

Good Practice In Supervision
Statutory and Voluntary Organisations
Edited by Jacki Pritchard
ISBN 1 85302 279 9 pb
Good Practice Series 2

Offering a new and much needed approach to supervision practice, *Good Practice in Supervision* considers the need and format for successful supervision, methods of effective implementation, particular difficulties and problems frequently encountered, and anti-discriminatory practice. Throughout the book, there are many practical suggestions and examples which complement the sound theoretical base of the text.

The contributors are drawn from a wide variety of settings, in both the voluntary and statutory sectors, and offer a range of approaches and perspectives. Discussion covers, among other topics, work with older people, court welfare supervision, students, and child protection. Such a thorough and important book addresses issues until now often overlooked.

CONTENTS: Introduction. *Jacki Pritchard.* 1. The Supervision Partnership. *Catherine Sawdon, Wakefield Social Services, and David Sawdon, Freelance Trainer.* 2. Taking Account of Feelings. *Elizabeth Ash, Consultant in Education and Training.* 3. Supervision in a Statutory Agency. *Paul Borland, South Yorkshire Probation Service.* 4. Supervision of Social Services Managers. *Patricia Riley, Wheatfields Hospice.* 5. Child Protection – Supervision within Social Services Departments. *Jean Moore, Child Abuse Consultant and Freelance Trainer.* 6. Supervision and Work with Older People. *Professor Cherry Rowlings, University of Stirling.* 7. Supervision of Home Care Staff. *Jacki Pritchard.* 8. Taking Supervision Work in Residential Care. *Roger Clough, University of Lancashire.* 9. Supervision in a Residential/Day Care Setting. *Dr Ron Wiener, Freelance Trainer and Community Psychologist.* 10. Supervision of Approved Social Work Practice. *Katherine Wiltshire, Indepedent Trainer and Consultant.* 11. Supervision and Appraisal in the Probation Service. *Hazel Kemshall, University of Birmingham.* 12. Supervising Staff in Family Court Welfare Teams. *Steve Mackey and Sue Lane, West Midlands Probation Service.* 13. Supervision in Probation and Bail Hostels. *Martin Roscoe, Hampshire Probation Service.* 14. Supervision in the Voluntary Sector. *Christine Stanners, Camden Age Concern.* 14. Supervision or Practice Teaching for Students? *Jacki Pritchard.*

Jessica Kingsley Publishers,
116 Pentonville Road, London N1 9JB

Good Practice in Child Protection
A Manual for Professionals
Edited by Hilary Owen and Jacki Pritchard
ISBN 1 85302 205 5 pb
Good Practice Series 1

'Each chapter is fully referenced, and some include case studies and exercises. I found *Good Practice in Child Protection* not only interesting but educational. It was harrowing to read the case studies and descriptions, and this shows the vital need of good training, supervision and support for workers in this field or for those who come into situations in which a child may be being abused in any way.'

– Nursing Standard

'will delight trainers. They could use the text as a pattern to mount immediate courses with stimulating exercises.'

– Community Care

Hilary Owen is Assistant Child Protection Co-ordinator at Sheffield Family and Community Services Department.

CONTENTS: Introduction, Hilary Owen and Jacki Pritchard. 1. Managing Your Own Learning in Child Protection, Ann Hollows *Senior Development Officer, National Children's Bureau.* 2. The Children Act and Child Protection, Pat Munroe *Solicitor.* 3. Recognition of Abuse, Dr Alice Swann *Senior Clinical Medical Officer, Belfast.* 4. Awareness and Recognition, Jo Crow *Sister in Accident and Emergency, The Children's Hospital, Birmingham.* 5. Recognition of Abuse by Workers in Other Specialisms, Jacki Pritchard. 6. Preventing Female Genital Mutilation: A Practical Multidisciplinary Approach, Hilary Owen and Lola Brown *Senior Race Relations Trainer (Child Protection), Lambeth Social Services.* 7. Children with Disabilities – A Challenge for Child Protection Procedures? Philippa Russell *Director, Voluntary Council for Handicapped Children.* 8. On Becoming a Tightrope Walker – Communicating Effectively With Children About Abuse, Eve Brock *Trainer & Team Leader of teachers, HM Prison Lindholme.* 9. Promoting Inter-Professional Understanding and Collaboration, Tony McFarlane *Multidisciplinary Training Officer, Co. Antrim.* 10. Developing Skills in Contributing at Child Protection Case Conferences, Hilary Owen and Lindsey Savage *Child Protection Administrator, Sheffield Family & Community Services Department.* 11.Child Protection Conferences: Maximising Their Potential, Marion Charles *Senior Lecturer, School of Social Studies, University of Nottingham.* 12. Formulating Child Protection Plans, Hilary Owen and Jacki Pritchard. 13. Victims of Child Abuse Giving Evidence: Helping to Reduce Trauma, Isobel Todd *Probation Officer, Nottinghamshire.* 14. Child Protection: The Police Perspective, Sergeant Colin Walke *Surrey Constabulary.* 15. Supervision and Support of Workers Involved in Child Protection Cases, Professor Dorota Iwaniec *Department of Social Work, Queen's University of Belfast.* 16. Support and Supervision for Social Workers Working in the Child Protection Field, Jacki Pritchard.

Jessica Kingsley Publishers,
116 Pentonville Road, London N1 9JB